HB

Down the Cobbled Stones

Down the Cobbled Stones

Memories of a Cheshire Farmer

John Lea

LARGE PRINT
Oxford

First published in Great Britain
as an illustrated book 1998
by
Churnet Valley Books

Published in Large Print 2005 by ISIS Publishing Ltd,
7 Centremead, Osney Mead, Oxford OX2 0ES
by arrangement with the author

British Library Cataloguing in Publication Data
Lea, John
    Down the cobbled stones. – Large print ed.
    – (Isis Reminiscence series)
    1. Lea, John
    2. Farmers – England – Cheshire – Biography
    3. Farm Life – England – Cheshire – History –
    20th cen Lea, John
    4. Polion   raphy
    5. Large Down the cobbled
    6. Chesh stones :   hy
    I. Title memories of a
    630.9'2   LP630.
                           1
         1652495

ISBN 0–7531–9300–0 (hb)
ISBN 0–7531–9301–9 (pb)

Printed and bound by Antony Rowe, Chippenham

ACKNOWLEDGEMENTS

My wife Celia for her help, encouragement,
and skill with a camera.
My sister Mary and brothers George and Arthur
for happily sharing their memories.

Harry Davies and the late Eric Davies.
Geoff Gough and the late Jim Gough.
Alan Richardson and Wenzel (Fred) Spatschek.

Each of them graciously shared their life memories with
me. My deep gratitude to them and to the many
relatives and friends who have filled in the gaps with
information and loaned me photographs, all usually
completed over a cup of tea and a piece of cake, in such
a friendly way as to make the writing of this book a
great pleasure.

My good friend G. Ashley Hunter has kindly
added a light touch of humour with some
special illustrations for the book, and for the cover.

CONTENTS

FOREWORD

By Lord Plumb MEP. Past President of the EEC
and the National Farmers Union

It is a privilege to write a foreword for John Lea's memoirs of his farming years. I can relive with him the nostalgic events that he so vividly portrays in his story of life among rural people in his native county of Cheshire.

I have always felt that I had an affinity with John, since some of his ancestors moved from Cheshire to Warwickshire at the same time as my grandparents. Farm tenancies were available and they were nearer the markets.

His account of hard times in the '20s and '30s will have a familiar ring to many of his readers who well remember those back-breaking days. "We had a half crown between us," John's father told him of how he cycled to Crewe market on two consecutive Mondays but did not spend it. John and Celia had bought their farm but his father's instructions were to keep a half crown for emergency, until money came in to put in the bank!

He tells us too of the suffering caused at Cheadle farm when disaster struck through the dreaded brucellosis. This created an enormous loss on many dairy farms throughout the country and I remember in my early days in the NFU being given the responsibility by Harold Woolley to persuade MAFF and Government to provide S.19 vaccine free and start a compulsory eradication scheme. The first Country Branch I visited after our success was naturally the premier dairy County of Cheshire when I was cut down to size by one of the then delegates. It was Jack Hough who said: "stuff can't be any good if they are giving it away."

John's account of the War years and the employment of Italian and German prisoners on the farm also brings back memories, since we also had a camp nearby. I remember looking across the benches on my first days in the European Parliament to see if I recognised any who had worked on our farms!

Tales of the characters, the real life of country folk who suffered the effects of the Depression in the early '30s, should be compulsive reading for young farmers and their families.

But John Lea himself is a real character. When he served on the Council of the NFU, I often said, "When John speaks, you listen." He was articulate, forthright and direct in his arguments and truly represented the feelings and concerns of family farmers. After his polio he had tremendous courage returning to his farm, a way of life he claims he couldn't live without.

It is difficult to compare the methods of farming and animal husbandry, so accurately described in this book, with the "agribusiness" of today, and it is difficult to plan ahead in such a volatile world. But these stories tell us that we must learn from History, and that we need people with the courage and conviction of John Lea if we are to maintain a living countryside for future generations.

INTRODUCTION

I was born into a farming family in the Depression but my parents prospered through it. Their sacrifice and determination brought them success, which in turn gave me a base for my own farming career. Although this book is based on the story of their life and mine, the real story is about the country people who lived and worked around my family.

I was always bored with history at school — having to learn a string of dates seemed pointless — but I have always been fascinated with people, particularly those who are part of my countryside. Although there is a little history in this book, it is not so much about facts or dates as about the people of that time; not just any people, but my people.

Many years ago a young Irishman came to work for me through the harvest season. After only a few days he mentioned someone who had worked for my father some years before, so I asked how did he know him. He gave some thought to his reply, and said, "Well, he's a — he's a — sort of a cousin." Many of the people in this book fit that delightful description.

The War brought Italian and German prisoners of war to share my home and my life. With an American camp by the farm which later housed prisoners of war from the Baltic countries — young men captured by the Germans and forced to wear German uniform — there were times when our farm was more like the United Nations. On one occasion there were eleven different nationalities working together in one field!

This book is my record of those many different people, and their stories told to me, some long ago, some recounted only recently. For Jim and Geoff Gough, Harry Davies, and many other relatives and friends who have contributed to these memories, this is their story. Memories are coloured through the years; I have been surprised how varied different people's accounts of the same event can be. This is my best attempt to relate those stories, as told to me, and as true to life as possible.

The story is set in the first half of this century in a group of villages around Lower Peover. Although they are in mid-Cheshire they could be almost anywhere in the Country. Farmers and village craftsmen, their work, their fun, their way of life; all of which was my inheritance and in turn became my way of life. Now it is time for me to share a little of it.

CHAPTER
ONE

Cheadle Farm

"We had a half-crown between us, and I cycled to Crewe cattle market two Mondays on the run, but I couldn't spend it." Those were the words of my father to me when my wife and I bought a farm of our own. He went on to say, "We kept it for emergency, because we dare not go near the bank until some money came in." He was trying to warn me that however careful I may have made my own farm budget, with livestock the unexpected can happen, and with animals, when the unexpected does occur it is usually costly.

At that time I had been married to Celia for three years; during those three years we had spent a lot of our time looking at different farms on the market, either to be let or for sale. Both of us were brought up on tenanted farms and we both had no wish to live any other kind of life. My father was prepared to retire and let us take over the farm, but the landlord was not prepared to discuss letting it until the farm became vacant. Dad had a life time tenancy and was not going to give his notice in on the chance that I might or might not get this tenancy. I was not prepared to live with that uncertainty so we decided to find a farm of our own.

We would have preferred to rent a farm, in fact we were shortlisted for one or two; we even refused one that we thought unsuitable. When it came to the final choice of tenant, the agent could not help but have doubts about my ability. I had polio when I was twenty, and although I could drive a tractor, I still walked with a stick and it was obvious that there were a lot of jobs on a farm which I couldn't do. We finally had to admit that no agent was likely to choose me if he had an alternative fit young man equally keen.

Our dream in 1965 was for a farm of about 250 acres, to run a herd of 100 dairy cows or more and have a mixed arable enterprise. The snag was that we had to borrow all the money to buy such a farm. We managed to convince our bank manager of our case, and we did eventually buy a farm with all borrowed money, but all of that is for a later story. This book is about my parents, the colourful characters that shared their country life with them, and my childhood.

To know what had influenced my father so much we have to go back many years to when they started farming. It was in 1929, during the long Depression, when they got the tenancy of a 40-acre Council farm in Goostrey, which lies in mid-Cheshire. The weather that winter had been very hard, with frosts most nights from late January through into early March. When my Father took possession of that farm in the March, normally all the fields to be cropped would have been ploughed ready for spring sowing, but he was faced with a farm where there had been no ploughing done at all. In fact the ground was so frozen that he couldn't plough until

2

early April. Even then, where the sun hadn't penetrated, there was still hard frozen soil beneath the surface. As he walked between the handles of a single-furrow plough pulled by a pair of horses, those frozen spots would jar his wrists and lift his plough up out of the ground.

The two horses that made up Dad's plough team were a present from his parents, my grand-parents, when he and Mother got the tenancy of Valley farm. They along with five cows were the base for my parents' farming future. Those two horses were Jewel, who was a mare with a lovely nature and the long graceful legs of a typical shire, and her partner, Prince, who was slightly smaller and thicker built but still had the shires' feathered legs. He was a gelding.

For the uninitiated, a gelding is a stallion that has had the cruellest cut — well, two cuts actually. I think Prince resented this interference with his private life because he was never quite as amenable as Jewel, but he was a willing worker and as a team they were my father's pride and joy.

My parents were only at Valley Farm for three years, but they must have been hectic years. My older brother George was born just prior to moving there, and my second brother Arthur and his twin sister Mary came along less than two years later. You can imagine how desperate my Father was to get some crops into the ground in that first year. Two strained wrists were a price that he was prepared to pay in his drive to raise the funds to finance the much needed investment in his new farm, and to provide for his young family.

3

Father often talked about that first Spring, and particularly about the frozen ground and how he ploughed over the deep patches of almost permafrost underneath. The soil was a very good and easily-worked loam. The frost had lifted it so that it came up in seedbed condition, needing very little harrowing before sowing or planting.

I don't know what he grew on that small farm but it must have been magic, because within three years he and Mother were on the move again to Cheadle Farm at Nether Peover, which is near Knutsford. The farm was on the boundary of Plumley, but within the parish of Lower Peover, and much of our life evolved around that parish. The church, the school, the blacksmith and the timber yard made Lower Peover an important village in that area.

The land at Cheadle Farm ran down to the Peover Eye. This lovely brook rises behind Gawsworth Hall and wends its way down through Chelford, giving its name to Over Peover, Lower Peover and a few other Peovers through which its tree lined banks meander as it flows across the Cheshire plain. This stream was noted for the quality of its trout fishing in the nineteenth century. Unfortunately pollution in the twentieth century prevented trout from breeding and caused its decline. I now have the pleasure of fishing a length of the Peover Eye, and in 1997 I caught a few small brown trout that had obviously been born in the stream — I believe the first for some fifty years.

It was a big step for my parents, to double their acres to eighty. Cheadle farm was typical of the small farms

4

in mid-Cheshire, with oak trees dotted along thick hawthorn hedges, but many of those hedges were overgrown and in need of attention. Most of the fields were about five to seven acres, although there was one three and a half acre field by the farmyard into which Jewel was turned in the years that she had a foal.

Producing a foal was part of my Dad's prudent farming policy and Jewel and her foal needed the full field to live off through the Summer grass-growing months. Horses are bad grazers in that they tend to graze some areas of a field and leave others untouched. Dad would turn some cows in occasionally, to eat off the parts that Jewel had left ungrazed but other than that it was the full three and a half acres just to keep one horse and her foal. On top of that it would need another acre or two to produce the hay needed to feed them through the winter. At the price that land is worth, it doesn't need a calculator to realise that keeping a horse is not the low cost system that some today would have us believe.

Part of this farm was heavy clay soil in permanent pasture, but there was still plenty of lighter, more easily worked ground in which to grow arable crops. To move to a new farm in the days of horses was a major operation, needing a lot of help from relatives and neighbours.

Dad had built his herd up from the original five to eighteen cows and these were all in-calf when they arrived at Cheadle Farm. But then disaster tragically struck in the form of brucellosis. The common name for brucellosis is contagious abortion, an appropriate

5

name because only two of Dad's eighteen cows had live calves that year, the others were all born premature and one of those two live calves died before it could go to market. In the neighbouring parish of Lach Dennis the outbreak was so bad that in that same year there were very few live calves born in the whole of the parish. When a cow aborts the calf is dead, and of course that is a financial loss, but the biggest loss is that the cow fails to produce a normal yield of milk, and often none at all.

It was that experience that made my parents so cautious and caused Father to warn me against being too optimistic. You may think it dramatic to say that in those few desperate weeks only a half-crown stood between them and failure, but it was a fact. Dad's farm had been in an outlying part of the Tabley Estate owned by Cuthbert Leycester Warren who sold the farms at public auction in 1920. Mrs Olive Battlesby bought Cheadle Farm for £7,100, and between then and my parents going to Cheadle Farm in 1929, three tenants came and went on the farm, two of them doing a moonlight flit. It may not be uncommon for a house tenant to flee in the night leaving debts unpaid, but a farmer with livestock and equipment has to be in a desperate strait to flee in the night.

There were two or three forced farm sales in the area most weeks, so for any farmer with some spare cash, secondhand machinery could be bought very cheap. It was in those hard years that Dad learned his bidding technique. Although a sale may have been caused by hardship and the family may have been in desperate need, he couldn't afford to pay a penny more than necessary. If a neighbour or friend wanted a machine or a cow at one of these sales, Dad knew it would cause offence to bid against them. Even if they managed to buy, they would always believe it would have been cheaper had Dad not bid. He developed a tiny movement of his thumb, just a little flick that auctioneers soon got to know, but it kept him out of any embarrassment throughout his farming life. In later years I have watched him leaning on the ringside rails, talking to another farmer who was obviously bidding, Dad's thumb flicking alternately to his bid. If the price got too high, Dad dropped out and no one but the auctioneer knew he had bid. If Dad's was the highest bid, when the auctioneer announced his name, the other man had to apologise for running Dad up!

My parents kept geese and hens and there were rabbits in the fields, so even with no money to spend, I am sure that there was still food on the table. The crisis lasted for most of a year, in fact it was not until the cows had calved again that they gave enough milk to return a reasonable milk cheque. During that time Mother learned how to cook the old hens that were too old to lay many eggs; she called them "boiling fowl". It was an appropriate name because to make them edible she would boil them for three or four hours and them roast them in the usual way. The end result was surprisingly good and these elderly hens were a part of our diet throughout my early life.

It was not until much later in my own life that I realised just how great the effect of that brucellosis outbreak had been. Dad was ill soon after and it went on for a while; in fact his neighbour John Clarkson had to help him, both with the milking and some of the field work. Doctors had not realised then that brucellosis could be passed on to humans so no diagnosis was made, but I am as sure as one can be that my Father suffered through his life from the lasting effects of that debilitating disease. Undulating fever is the medical term for the human form of brucellosis, and its effect on people can be quite varied. Dad was never able to do heavy work for any length of time. If he joined in heavy work he would soon tire and make some excuse to go to see to his business elsewhere on the farm. I suspect that he had a temper before this illness (well, I inherited mine from someone!), but the undulating effect of this disease made him more erratic and more prone to outbursts of frustrated temper. They were the down side to a quite remarkable farmer. The condition didn't in any way dampen his ambition, and perhaps by making him walk away from continuous hard physical work it gave him time to think and plan.

It is hard for us to realise how basic life was just that short time ago. There was no hot water system, or even running water. The first one down in a morning lit the fire and put the kettles on. There was no hot water until they had warmed up, and a freshly lit fire takes a while to boil a kettle. The second job in Dad's day was to get the milking finished in time to catch the milk train from Plumley station. It was not just a matter of doing the milking but the milk had to be cooled if it was to keep fresh on the slow journey into Manchester.

8

Then there was also the transport to the station. A pony or light horse was kept on each farm for this purpose. It would also be used by the family, perhaps for going to market and to Church or Chapel on Sunday. This pony would be harnessed and in the shafts of a light cart ready to dash to the station the moment the last milk tankard was put into it. The actual milking was not so physically demanding as today, when in modern milking parlours one man may milk up to two hundred cows and by the end feel as though he has run a marathon. Then each person would sit on a stool whilst he or she milked between five and seven, with the odd hardy soul milking up to ten cows.

The train deadline made each morning a time fraught with tension. Dad's good friend and neighbour John Clarkson got into the habit each morning of standing next to his pony whilst his two men lifted the last tankard of milk into the milk float. When it landed in the float, one man would fasten the rear door whilst the other leapt up on the front to grab the reins and hang on. John Clarkson was standing by with a twitch raised, and as his man got hold of the reins, John would bring it down with a thwack on the pony's rump. The air of tension and excitement around one morning, when the operation was behind time, must have been communicated to the horse — or perhaps the thought of the raised twitch got to it. When the last milk churn landed in the float the horse beat the twitch and headed for the station — but without his driver. With no one on board to calm it down, the horse made good time that morning. Unfortunately the back door was still undone and the milk tankards bounced out one by one and decorated the country lane an expensive colour of white.

The light cart used on this mad morning run was usually called a shandrey. It was made to carry only about five hundredweight and could be pulled by a light horse or strong pony. On dairy farms it was known as the milk float; the same cart often carried the calves to market and was then sometimes called the calf float. On the small farms where they could not afford a trap, the farmer would use that same cart for the family — I don't know what it was called then.

That frantic dash to the station ended soon after Dad went to Cheadle Farm. Motor transport was coming into operation then, but there was still a collection deadline to beat. The other major improvement to the lot of dairy farmers was the arrival of the Milk Marketing Board in 1933. The MMB bought and collected all the milk of each farm, selling the milk on to many small dairies; it then pooled the proceeds to pay one standard price to the farmers. Before the MMB, Dad had to go to Manchester and negotiate his own milk sale. In fact he had to go from buyer to buyer until he found one willing to take his milk, and even then there were many days when the dairy did not want his milk for whatever reason, when a postcard would come with the instruction to keep his milk at home the next day. This milk would have to be made into butter, which put a heavy burden on Mother in the house.

Payment for milk was also very uncertain in those pre-MMB days. Now after sixty years of successful trading a Conservative government has done away with it in the name of privatisation. Pool pricing has gone with the MMB and I fear that it will be the end of many smaller and remote farms.

In the early years at Cheadle Farm, Dad needed at least two men to help him with the work (he never said how he managed to pay them through that bad year). In 1933 a top teamsman's wage was 33s per week, for which at peak times he could work up to 60 hours. Even so, my father couldn't afford someone on that wage. His staff at first was a youth "living in" on about 10s a week with his board on top, and Jimmy, who was Irish and lived in a shant on the farm — one room with a small fireplace, bed, table and chair.

Breakfast time came at the end of morning milking, and by then the kettles would be boiling and the men could wash and shave. Mother had a little paraffin stove on which she cooked the home cured bacon, not only for our own family but for the staff that "lived in" with the family. Mains water only came to that area in the mid-thirties. Before then, water was hand-pumped up from the well. Mother had a busy life with three young children, plus staff to feed, handwashing of clothes, and churning unsold milk into butter. To do all this she had a teenage girl to help her, Phyllis who lived in the farmhouse. Phyllis helped with the milking each morning, then she and Mother would feed the hens, ducks, geese and give support to most of the farm's activities.

11

Breakfast was a busy time in the house, so Jimmy made his own breakfast in his shant, but his technique was a bit unusual. With only a thirty minute break there was no time for him to light a fire. He knew Mother would have a kettle boiling so Jimmy would bring his brew can to the door and at the same time buy two eggs. When Mum handed him his brew can back, he would turn his back on her so that she couldn't see (as he thought) and pop the eggs into the tea. I presume that he declared them cooked when he got back to his shant.

Looking after himself, Jimmy bought economically, and a sheep's head at a penny or two came within his budget. The fireplace was small so the saucepan was not very large and a whole sheep's head wouldn't fit in it. Jimmy solved the problem by cooking one side and eating that; then he turned it over to cook and ate the other side. Phyllis went round to his shant one evening and was faced with a sheep seemingly looking at her out of a saucepan. She was sick on the spot. After that if anyone mentioned sheep's head she would be sick. One night a few weeks later, she was smartly dressed and waiting by the road side for her boyfriend. Just as he came up the road towards her, the farm lad shouted "sheep's head, Phyllis", and the poor girl was immediately sick again.

Phyllis got her own back on Jimmy, though. Most stables had a loose box attached, where a sick horse or perhaps one that was going to foal could be kept. The door into ours was from within the stable. When not needed for a horse, Father kept a sow and litter in

12

there. One particular sow was savage and poor Jimmy was very frightened of her, but it was his job to clean her out each day. To do this he kept his brush between himself and the pig, and with his back to the door he would carefully pull the muck back through the door. Even then the sow would rush at him but he could just about hold her off with the brush.

Phyllis crept up when he was reaching into the loose box and shut the door behind him. The fasten was on the outside and Jimmy couldn't open it. Dad eventually heard strange noises and went to investigate. Jimmy dared not shout in case he provoked the sow into a more ferocious attack and by the time Dad rescued him he was near breaking point, pleading in vain for Phyllis to let him out — but Phyllis had long gone back into the farm house. When Dad opened the door, Jimmy was backed up against it, shaking with fear as he fended the enraged sow off with his brush.

It was tradition on Cheshire farms for staff to "live in" the farmhouse. On some farms they lived very much as family, sharing home, food and company. On others they were kept firmly in their place, eating in a separate room, and sleeping in a separate part of those large farm houses. Some farms in Cheshire made most of their milk into cheese, selling only the surplus to the MMB. Those cheese making farms needed a lot of workers, and on some there were five or six youths and the same number of girls "living in" on the one large farm.

When Celia and I were looking for a farm in the mid-sixties, we saw some interesting old farm houses.

In one large farmhouse at Arley, which did not seem to have been altered for over a hundred years, there were three staircases; a grand stairway for the master and his family, a back staircase that went up to the attic for the servant girls, and then to keep the boys apart from the girls, an enclosed spiral staircase leading up to a completely separate set of attic bedrooms. There was no dividing door between boys and girls or any way through, other than by coming down to the ground floor and climbing the other stairs — and they went past the master bedroom to do that. Teenagers were still teenagers a hundred years ago so I have often wondered what method was used to overcome the problem. I am sure some of them would have knotted a sheet or climbed a downspout, or done something even more creative to get together. These young people would move on when they got married, perhaps into a tied cottage on the same farm, or they might have to move further away to find employment.

The time when young people "lived in" was a period of apprenticeship for them. The lads would learn the skills of farming, and the girls would learn both farm and dairy skills, and for many there was the added experience of running a large farm house. Of course there were often the farmer's own children and marriage was not uncommon between staff and the son or daughter of the farmer. Sometimes there was the heartbreak when the farmer father thought the match was not in their class and broke up the relationship. There were also many instances where a servant girl

14

never married but stayed on with, and became part of, that same farming family throughout her life.

You may be wondering if Celia and I bought that large farm house. Well no, I think Celia put me off when she suggested that to run a house that size, she also would need about four servant girls.

The mid-1930s was a time of change, with new thinking within agriculture and a growing interest in the countryside by people outside agriculture. It was in 1935, after several events of mass trespass, that the formation of the Ramblers Association took place. About then and leading up to the War, there were signs that the Country was slowly beginning to climb out of Depression. It is always said that "farming is the last into depression and the last out". This one followed that pattern. For example, wheat prices in 1934 were the lowest during the Depression. The length and severity of it had left farmers badly bruised financially, and those that survived very cautious with money.

Those were eventful years in the history of farming not just because the industry was coming out of a long and stagnating period, but also because artificial fertiliser began to make an impact on crop production. It was in 1937 that the Agricultural Act introduced subsidies for the application of lime and basic slag, although they were already in use on many farms. Through the worst of the Depression quite a lot of land had not been farmed or had only been ranched with beef cattle. This happened when landlords could not find a suitable tenant who was prepared to take on the farm. They would then leave the land to go derelict, or run a few beef cattle on it, to eat some of the grass, and make do best they could. That left the hedges uncut and the ditches and drains to deteriorate. In the end to encourage a tenant to take on such a farm, it would have to be offered rent free for the first year. Those farms needed phosphate from basic slag, and lime to correct the pH, if grassland productivity was to be improved. Subsidising those two inputs was to give production a much needed long term boost.

The same Act also brought in deficiency payments for barley and oats. Those relatively small subsidies brought a much needed price stability to some of the arable crops, giving farmers that little more confidence to invest. To illustrate just how low food production had got before the War, the population of the country was a little over half of what it is now, but we produced less than half of the food needed to feed them. The import bill for that amount of food drained our balance of payments to such an extent that the government, aware of the threat of war, had become desperate to increase food production. Manufacturing industry turns over its working capital about every three months; farmers turn their working capital over in about three years. To invest over that length of time they needed confidence, and deficiency payments gave them a feeling of security. Now towards the end of the twentieth century this country produces over eighty per cent of its own food, a massive increase to our national budget and a benefit to every member of the population.

The Government may have woken up to the need to bolster farming, but the farmers still had to contend with nature and their dependence on the horse. It is difficult for our generation to realise how hard it was then to overcome difficult spells of weather with the machinery of that time. Working a seed bed with just horses and harrows was a time consuming operation. If the weather was unsettled it was impossible to predict a long enough spell of dry weather needed to get a crop in. It had taken Dad five days to plough five acres with two horses and it would take him another five days with the same two horses to harrow a seedbed, and sow and roll the same field. Dad had "worked the field down" (our description of a seedbed ready to sow); it was one of our more heavy soils. Unfortunately there was a heavy rain storm before he could sow the oat seed on it. The clay soil turned to porridge and it was weeks before there was enough sunshine to dry it out. Dad still put his oats in but by then it was late in the season. That field only yielded the same weight at harvest time as the seeds when they were sown in spring.

That crop failure dictated the pace of his life each spring, and in years to come mine also, because he was determined that never again would he be caught with a soggy, unsown seedbed. When it was time to sow he would be watching his old barometer. When he believed there was a good chance of settled weather, all the horses and machinery would be set to work in just one field. They would work up to the limit of each horse each day until the seeds were sown. It was only when that field was near completion that he would decide if he dare start some of his team working in another field.

The MMB was proving to be a revolution to Cheshire dairy farmers in that it took all the milk each farmer could produce. My father continued to grow potatoes and cereals and even kept some sheep and pigs, but he saw the potential of milk production. At last there was a market for a product with no limit to production and above all a guaranteed payment day each month. Cows were tied up in "shippens" (I describe them in the next chapter) and still milked by hand. So there was, in fact, a limit to Father's milk production, but it was created by the lack of buildings to house cows in, and to a lesser extent by how many cows one pair of hands could milk at a session. More hands could be hired, but landlords, who had also been drained of resources through the recession, were very reluctant to put up the expensive buildings needed for tenants to house more cows through the winter months.

Dad bought his first car at this time, a secondhand Humber-Siddeley, and it must have completely changed both our family life and our farming business. Of course, up to then my brothers and sister had walked to and from Lower Peover school, and being enterprising children they now fancied a lift. Dad being an expert at bargaining, soon struck a deal. He would give them a lift to school if they got up early and helped him with the milking first. This they did. Of course the children would be allowed to milk the quiet and easily milked cows. Arthur's boast was that he had milked his first cow the night he was six. In fact some years later when I was struggling to milk my first cow at the ripe old age of seven, he stood just behind me repeating the tale of his exploit. I would have tipped the milk over him — but I was too afraid of Father.

CHAPTER
TWO

Horse Power

Dad was convinced of the need to have many different enterprises on his farm. It was his hope that at least one would make a profit and, without the specialised and expensive equipment needed today, a man with a fork and shovel could work with any animal. A small flock of sheep were part of his very mixed farm and our few ewes were put to a Suffolk ram. That ram was a bit unusual in that he not only had been an orphan lamb hand-fed by children, but also at some stage he must have been allowed to suckle a small cow. None of this was known to Dad when he bought him in the market, but it was soon obvious when he got out of his own field into the cows. Not just once but repeatedly — in fact any herd of cows would do.

At the same time he did not like men. If Dad or any of his staff were working in the same field as the tup, he would be after them all the time. A fully grown tup charging head down from twenty or thirty yards distance comes at some speed and is a very dangerous beast to handle. Dad worked out a method of action. When the tup charged, right at the last moment he would step to one side, grab a hold of its wool and tip it over. Not an easy thing to do with two hundred and fifty pounds of enraged mutton charging at speed. If Dad got it wrong and stepped aside too soon the tup would swerve like a rugby player and then it was Dad who got turned over. Even when the tup had been rolled over, the mad thing would be straight up and after Dad again unless he had a piece of string ready in his pocket. When he was fencing or working near the tup, it had to lie with its legs tied together until the job was done!

On one occasion Jimmy didn't hear the tup coming up behind him and it hit him a terrible blow, knocking him through a thick thorn hedge into the next field, where he lay bruised and winded. When poor Jimmy got his breath back and tried to get up, he found that the tup had jumped through after him and was, somewhat sportsman like, waiting for him to get to his feet before charging again. Jimmy must have held a grudge because a little later that summer, when Dad was shutting his hens in for the night, he found the tup lying neatly trussed up. Had the tup not been released, its stomach would have filled with gas and it would have been dead before morning. Jimmy was by then drinking its health (or more likely its demise) in the local pub. When he came home he declared that "he had just forgotten the poor thing".

The tup remained on good terms with my brothers. If he heard them playing around the farm he would usually try to join them; he would bash through a fence or jump a ditch to be with them. When George was learning to ride his bike along the lane the tup joined him. As he peddled away on his little bike the tup galloped alongside, but it eventually got a bit too close and tipped him off into the ditch. Unfortunately for George the ditch took the dirty water from the farmyard and a very wet and very smelly George ended up having to be washed off in the tin bath in front of the kitchen fire.

The dirty water came from where the dairy cows were housed and milked. They were tied by the neck in a stall, usually in a double stall with a "boskin" between every second cow. This "boskin" was not just a division but was also the anchor for the neck chain that held each cow in its stall. The building that the cows were housed in we Cheshire farmers called a "shippen". Inside it the stalls were side by side in a long row with a low wall in front of them, and beyond that low wall was the "fodderbing", where the hay and other food was kept for ease of feeding each cow. It was the warmest place on the farm, a dosshouse for tramps in the winter, and often used by youths in the winter evenings for a game of cards or other activities. Perhaps the Arley farmhouse young people did not need to climb down or up drain spouts because on cold winter nights it was often warmer in the "shippen fodderbing" than in the farmhouse.

Some years later a cattle food salesman told me how he had just called at a nearby farm. He hadn't found the farmer around the yard and was about to drive away when he heard a giggle. He then took a look in the shippen where he found two of the farmer's daughters, each with her boyfriend snuggled down in the soft hay at opposite ends of the cosy fodderbing.

In their stalls each cow lay on a raised concrete "bed" which was covered with straw. There was a "groupin" behind them, some six inches lower and about two feet wide, to catch the dung. Then at the back of that was the "walk", raised about four inches above the "groupin" which was the pathway for the cowman to attend to each cow. The dung was cleaned out twice each day with a shovel and wheelbarrow. There were some double shippens where the cows stood back to back, sharing one walk, but most of them at that time were single shippens holding about ten to fifteen cows each.

This meant that a farm with thirty cows would have three separate shippens and in them the dairy herd was housed for over half the year; through the winter months from mid October until May 7th. A few years after the water mains had come to the farm it was possible to provide a drinking bowl for each cow. Before that the cows were turned loose in the yard each morning. That served three purposes, it allowed them to drink at the farm pond or stream, it gave the cowman chance to clean and re-straw the stalls, and equally importantly it allowed the farm bull to wander in amongst them to attend to his business. As cows usually stay on heat for twenty four hours, that hour each morning was enough to get them all in calf again.

Through the Summer months the herd was out eating grass, but they still had to come back to the shippens twice each day to be milked. Each cow knew its own stall, but of course each one didn't go straight to it, each would want to look in one or two other stalls just in case there was a bit of food left lying around. But if you made the mistake of tying one in the wrong stall, within ten minutes it could be leaping around and making a fuss. Each milking time was a confusion of milling cows, needing to be sorted into the right shippen and then into the right stall within it.

One day one of Father's neighbours sent an urgent message, asking him to come quickly because of the tup. By then Dad had bought a half share in a cattle trailer along with his friend John Clarkson, so Dad and my young brothers hooked it behind the car and went off to visit our neighbour. Although it was milking time and there was the usual confusion of cows wandering around in their farmyard, this time the farm staff were not sorting them out. The men were in fact hiding behind doors because the tup having thumped one of them, was stalking around the yard looking for another victim. Dad backed the trailer in to the yard but stayed out of the way, and the neighbour and his men didn't dare venture out. All watched from their protection as my two brothers dealt with the tup. They were only six and eight years old but they had no trouble in persuading that massive (alongside them) animal to walk tamely into the trailer.

That was the end for Dad. The tup sired a good type of lamb and for that reason it was really too good to kill, so he took it to Crewe Market and sold it. He declared the fault and the buyer assured him that he could handle it, but only a few weeks later, it escaped across the fields to another farmer's herd of cows. The cowman came to collect them for milking completely unaware of any danger; he was charged and had his leg broken.

About this time Harry Davies came to work on the farm. He had in fact been born in the same farmhouse as my Dad next to Granage Mill at Holmes Chapel. Harry's Father had followed my Grandad there; he ran the small farm along with a thrashing machine contracting business. He died when Harry was still at school and Harry's two much older stepbrothers took over the contracting business. My Grandfather, and my Father's two youngest, still unmarried brothers, then farmed Mrs Davies's land and housed cattle in the farm buildings through the winter months. Harry spent all his spare time with them helping, not only on his mother's farm but also on my Grandfather's farm nearby. In winter after school he would often help to water the cattle that were tied up in the shippens at his home. There was no running water so they were watered with buckets filled from the well by a hand pump; both very heavy jobs for a schoolboy, but he enjoyed it and had no wish to do anything but farming when he left school.

Harry "lived in" and worked for Dad for many years. During that time he became noted for being a very good teamsman, and I am indebted to him for helping with these memories. The farm that was his mother's is now built over with houses, but he and two of his sisters bought one of them, and his brother Eric and his wife managed to buy another. They all now live in houses that were built on their parents' land.

It was common for boys to help on local farms after school, at weekends and through holidays. Their knowledge of farming and livestock when they left school was exceptional. At thirteen they surpassed most of today's children who leave school at eighteen, and because of that they were often given responsibility beyond their years. Now at the turn of the twenty-first century the size, power and complexity of machinery on our farms make them a dangerous place. If today's children wanted to work like Harry did, or even just to spend time with the men on a farm, I doubt whether a farmer dare let them. Harry loved the farm life and after he left my Dad to live in Holmes Chapel, he worked until retirement on Cranage Hall Farm.

Although I have used the term "teamsman", it was not used on Cheshire farms, here we called them "horsemen" or "waggoners". To confuse you more we called our heavy four-wheeled waggons a lorry. They were flat topped with heavy iron-rimmed wooden wheels. Lads coming to work on a farm would be watched carefully by the farmer. Every boy wanted to be a "waggoner" but few had the natural gift with horses to be successful. It was not something that could be taught but a natural affinity with horses which could be built on to make such a lad into a good horseman.

Ponds were the only source of drinking water in most fields on the farm. Although the Peover Eye ran along the bottom of the farm it only provided water on those bottom fields. The fields between them and the farm buildings still relied on the old Cheshire ponds. Some of them were naturally created by the action of an ancient glacier that passed this way in the Ice Age. Large boulders of ice must have rolled along the bottom of the glacier and they became buried in the mud and sand as the glacier retreated. When the temperature warmed up those large blocks of ice melted leaving many deep holes on our flat Cheshire plain. Those that held water became ponds, many of them not large, but some very deep indeed.

Other ponds in our County were man-made. For many centuries our farmers were convinced that to spread marl was beneficial to crops. They were so convinced of the benefit of this natural mixture of clay and lime, that as far back as the reign of both Edwards I and II, leases contained clauses obliging tenants to use marl as manure. Although marl could be found throughout the County, it was only in small blocks, generally no more than some twenty five yards across and perhaps ten yards in depth. It was probably laid down by the same glacier action that left the ponds, because marl was often lying on a bed of gravel or sand and under a few feet of clay. The clay that lies under many parts of the County is nearly as hard as concrete. It must have been back-breaking work removing it by hand, then digging the marl, loading it onto carts and spreading it over the ground. Many of our fields show evidence of this work and some of our ponds were created that way. The fact that marl was in relatively small concentrations explains why it was dug in seemingly strange places, such as out in the middle of a field.

It was in one of those ponds that Prince had got stuck, and no amount of horsemanship could make Jewel pull her mate when she thought that she was hurting him. It had been a dry Summer and the water was low, exposing more mud than usual. Prince had perhaps gone in to cool off. Whatever the reason, he was down to his neck in the water and of course his feet were stuck right down in the mud. Dad and his staff dug the bank away in front of Prince and then harnessed Jewel into the cart, and backed it up to the very lip of the pond. They then tied a rope around the neck of Prince and to the axle of the cart. Their idea was that the height of the axle would help to lift Prince as well as pull. This is not as dangerous as one may think because when the rope tightened, the horse would rear back and thrash out with his front legs, freeing them from the mud. Then with only a steady pull on the rope the hope was that Prince would almost climb out himself.

I can imagine the anxiety around that pond. Prince was more important to Dad than any member of his staff, so he wouldn't spare their feelings (or even their lives for that matter). He would have fired out orders as he dashed from one spot to another. When all was set up he gave the order to pull, but when the rope tightened on Prince he whinnied in fear and Jewel stopped. No coaxing, or tricks of horsemanship, could make her pull her lifelong companion when she thought she was hurting him. In the end Dad sent a man across the fields to our neighbours for one of their horses. I bet he had his orders about not dallying on the way, but even so it would take some time to catch, harness and walk with the horse by the road back to our farm. It all ended well. I have no doubt that Prince would have had to be cleaned up, but he had no lasting ill effects.

Although there were many other horses through the years, these two were the main power of his farming life, through until tractors took their place in the later years of the War. Perhaps because of that, I should break my story to tell you a little about horses. Not just about farmhorses, because the heavy horse was also the source transport power in our Country up to the early part of this century. It is believed that the present day heavy horse descended from two groups that survived the last Ice Age. They developed in what is now called northern Europe where lush pasture interspersed with thick forest meant that they did not have to travel far for food. This abundance of grazing allowed those indigenous horses to develop into heavy and slow-moving animals. Of these the Flemish horses had the most influence in the ancestry of most European breeds and particularly our own Shire and Clydesdale breeds. Remains of horses found in the Ardennes region indicate that heavy horses have lived in that region since prehistoric times. It is surprising then to realise that their use in farming is restricted to the last few hundred years.

Today's public seem to have a romantic view of what life was like with horses. Horse-power meant a powerful horse — often with an unpredictable temperament. These so-called "gentle giants" are bred from wild animals which for millions of years have had to fight to survive. They could and still can kill with hoof or jaws; as children growing up with them on the farm we were taught to fear them. Just as their ancestors fought off wolves with a wicked back kick, so today's horse instinctively uses the same method to see off the farm collie. We were never allowed into the stable as young children. A horse might catch a glimpse of a child through the corner of its eye, think it is a dog and "bang". Most farming families could relate how this or that child was "flattened" against the stable wall, often by the supposedly "quiet" horse.

Their greatest weapon was their ability to run. Being a herd animal, if one ran, they all ran. To flee from danger was instinctive; if one horse fled there was obviously danger, so it was equally instinctive for the rest of the herd to flee with him. Millions of years of in-built genetic instinct is not erased in a few hundred years, and that natural reaction has given many teamsmen a shock through the years. Just a horse galloping around in a field next to the road could trigger a like response in a passing team. If ever one horse ran away down the road, then every teamsman on that road would have to dash to get a firm grip of his own horse's bridle. If he was too slow, his own horse or team could easily be following the runaway.

The sheer power of a horse had the potential to kill as Father found out at Valley Farm. Jewel was the most gentle of horses, yet she was involved in the worst

30

accident ever on our farm. A sixteen year old boy was leading her from the cornfield; Jewel knew the way and didn't really need to be led, so the lad just walked alongside her, with the large iron hooped wheels of the cart well behind him. Either he slipped and fell or he just slowed his walking pace; whichever, the iron rimmed cartwheel caught his heel, ran up his body and off just below his shoulder. He got up and walked away seemingly unhurt only to collapse at his home the following day with a ruptured spleen.

In the Middle Ages heavy horses were used for war and were bred mainly to carry heavy armour. Then towards the end of Henry VIII's reign their role began to change. It was not until after about 1600 that the use of horses to haul heavy wagons around the Country became popular — and the war horse became the draught horse. Before then oxen had been used for farmwork and a lighter built packhorse was the carrier of goods across country. Those packhorse routes went up and down banks, over mountains rather than round them. Above Macclesfield the ancient packhorse routes often had steps in the steeper lengths. But they were not the type of road for the heavy draught horse.

Horses slowly took over from oxen on the farms, but oxen could still be found working on some farms right up to the end of the nineteenth century. The heavy horse only dominated the farming seen for about 250 years and was bred from a mixture of imports, particularly the black Flemish from the Low Countries, the predominant ancestor of both the Shire and the Clydesdale. They developed along different lines to converge again now into one breed. The breed societies have encouraged the emphasis on uniformity of traits in the last hundred years; before then there was much more variance in type and in my Father's day working horses were a strange mixture of types and breeds. The horse of his day was shorter in the leg and thicker in build than today's shire. Many farmers thought that this shape of horse was the strongest when working in the shafts of a cart.

One stallion could have a considerable impact within a breed, on both the shape and size of that breed. Breeders would send mares from a wide area to mate with a popular sire. He would be fed on a rich diet that included raw eggs and milk and often in the breeding season such a stallion would cover a mare every thirty minutes, some times on through the night. The owner of that energetic animal would receive a fee on service, and a second fee when the mare was proved in foal. Those in total could run into many thousands of pounds per year. The best of his male foals would in turn be used at stud spreading his bloodline throughout the Country. At the same time I am sure that such a proof of prowess encouraged the consumption of raw eggs and milk among the envious onlookers!

Next to our farm was a smallholding, farmed by "Old Man" Bell, (he was always known by that addition to his name). Mr Bell was badly handicapped with rheumatism, the country people blaming this on his habit when young of ignoring wet weather and continuing to work through heavy showers, letting his clothes dry on his back. That, and sitting on damp ground were always said to be the cause of rheumatism. When we were children Mother would treat it as one of the most deadly sins; if we were caught perched on some comfortable hedge-cop with nothing under our bottoms, we had a severe reprimand.

Perhaps Old Man Bell didn't have such a caring mother because in his old age he was reduced to walking with two sticks. That must have been a big disadvantage to him when trying to make a living from a few acres. Most of the smaller farmers needed to supplement their income by other work of some kind. They either did casual work on nearby larger farms, or had a more regular job with the many small rural businesses that served the farming community. Mr Bell's handicap ruled him out of any of that work off the farm and even made it increasingly hard for him to manage his own small farm. His thatched cottage was in bad repair, after a strong wind he could be seen struggling up a ladder to replace some thatch that had blown off. Unfortunately it is nearly impossible to repair thatch like that; the only way is to strip off the thatch above the hole right to the ridge and replace all that block, or better still re-thatch the whole roof. I suppose this was more than Mr Bell could afford, so he was reduced to continuously patching the thatch and also keeping a few buckets handy inside to catch the drips.

The other problem, with farming on an insufficient income, is how to replace worn-out equipment. In Old Man Bell's case it was his horse that had to be replaced and the best he could afford was a mule, and even that was quite mad. Donkey Warberton supplied the mule. He was a man of many parts (we will return to him later in the story), he dealt in horses and had a knacker's yard near to Altrincham. He came into our life in Plumley because he also owned a small farm in the parish. The horses he supplied were noted for being a bit dodgy and this mad mule was one of them. Well, it wasn't even a mule because they are bred out of a mare by a donkey stallion — I believe that Old Man Bell's was bred the other way round and so it was a "Jennet", a foal out of a donkey mare by a horse stallion. I am not sure that I could tell the difference, but the old horsemen of that time knew at a glance.

It was not the recommended cross for two reasons; firstly the danger that the foal sired by a larger horse would be too large at birth for the donkey, and secondly they were often mentally unstable. The birth of such an animal would not have been planned, more than likely a donkey mare would have been out at grass and come in season without the farmer realising it. A stallion would get her scent in the breeze, even if he was in a field some distance away. With nothing better to do than eat grass, a quick foray over a couple of fences to meet a lady would pass the time quite nicely. Mules were not the brightest of animals at the best but a Jennet was even worse. This one got into our field where the ewes and lambs were peacefully grazing, and galloping in amongst them it picked a lamb up in its mouth and shook and killed it like a dog with a rat.

To make a small farm pay, it was necessary to grow some of the more intensive crops. For Mr Bell those

34

consisted of mostly potatoes and vegetables, with some soft fruit and fruit trees in the orchard to increase the sales in late Summer. For that work Old Man Bell had to rely on his mad Jennet to pull the small cultivator and drill plough in amongst the growing crops. A mule could be good for that type of work; being smaller than a horse it could turn in tight areas and its small feet did less damage than those of a large shire horse. Unfortunately, that one's erratic behaviour more that cancelled out those benefits. Not only was it hard to control in amongst the growing crops, it also used to bash into Mr Bell when he was trying to harness it, sometimes even knocking him down. Some said that the Jennet had been sent to Donkey Warberton's to be put down because it was so stupid. Like all horse dealers he was always out to make a pound or two, so he didn't put it down but persuaded Mr Bell to buy it "very cheap".

Old Man Bell died whilst we were at Cheadle Farm, and Harry Davies, dressed in his best suit, drove Prince in the light lorry to the little thatched cottage and from there took Old Man Bell on his last journey to Lower Peover Church. Prince was a good shaft horse, being nearly black with a long white blaze down his face, and with his looks and steady walk he would add dignity to any funeral. Although Harry himself could not remember the funeral, other members of my family could recall it clearly, particularly the quiet peace of the slow funeral cortege behind Prince.

The small farmer had to make do with what horse power he could afford. Those who worked part time for larger farmers often borrowed the boss's team for heavy work such as ploughing. At other times each would have the beast or beasts he had managed to buy; I say "beasts" because it could be horse, pony, bullock, mule, donkey or usually a combination of any of them. The working bullock was seldom seen in the twentieth century. In the past it wasn't uncommon for a smallholder to have a bullock to pull his small cart, plus a light horse to both ride and also to use for working in the fields — even on occasions to hitch them both together for a heavy job.

But transport was moving from horse to motor lorry in the 1930s. That had a dramatic effect on the lives and the business of all country people; from being tied to having to deal with the nearest shop or water mill, suddenly alternatives were available. Even the local blacksmith came under competition from travelling farriers.

What we forget is that all the new machinery also needed people to drive and work it. Most country people had little or no knowledge of engines or mechanics. Netty Ulse was a cousin of my Mother's and lived in the next parish of Allostock and, like most of my relatives, her family was involved in farming but her father and brother were wheelwrights. Netty proudly cycled out to Cheadle Farm with her boyfriend Reg Frith who, although coming from a farming family, had served his apprenticeship with his future father-in-law as a wheelwright. Reg had never driven a car and fancied having a drive in an old Morris Pick-up which had been left for my Father to try out on the

36

farm. To describe it as a pick-up might mislead you because it was quite small. The box on the back was not much larger than a good sized window box. Dad drove it into the meadow next to the farm buildings and left it running for Reg to have his first drive.

When that field had been last ploughed it had been done in butts and reans, which gave the meadow an undulating effect that was not the best surface to drive over. For those of you who do not know what butts and reans are, perhaps I should explain. It was a method of ploughing heavy clay soil to create surface drainage when the field was seeded down to permanent pasture. Light sandy soil allowed water to soak through more quickly so there was no need to plough that type of soil that way. The butt was made by ploughing the first furrow over onto the top of the ground. Then turning back from the opposite end, the waggoner ploughed a second furrow to over lap the first one; if the waggoner was ploughing six inches deep this would in effect create a mound twelve inches high. The waggoner would then, with careful measurement, plough a similar butt parallel to the first, the distance between the two varied from farm to farm but was often about five yards. The horseman would then plough between the two butts, turning the soil to the right butt as he went up the field and to the left one as he came back down. After a few rounds those furrows would meet in the middle, creating a hollow which became the rean. When harrowed and seeded with grass, the difference in contour between the butt and rean could be over a foot, that gave a nice slope for water to run of the tops of the butts and into the reans. The fields were ploughed so that there was fall down the reans, which made them into mini-brooks in heavy rain; in fact a few centuries ago that is what the word "rean" meant.

There is a down side to this system though, and that became quickly evident to me years later when I drove a tractor across them. It was in my school holidays. It was an old Fordson and after half a day harrowing I came home across a pasture ploughed that way. Those tractors only had three gears, and that particular one had been used on an airport and had a very high top gear. The result was either a tediously slow journey in second gear, or a much more exhilarating one in top gear. For a schoolboy it wasn't even a choice! The seat on that old tractor was mounted on a long spring steel arm that came up and out from the rear of the tractor some three to four feet and was between my legs as I sat on the metal seat. With no more than a folded empty corn sack to protect my bottom it was remarkably comfortable.

When I hit the butts and reans in top gear it was like being on a trampoline. Over each butt I rose a little higher from the seat, and just managed to hold onto the steering wheel and land back on the now uncovered metal seat each time. I needed desperately to slow down but the accelerator was a hand lever, low down to the right, completely out of my high-flying reach. I made an extra effort to reach it, which landed me in an untidy heap forward of the seat and straddling the three inch wide spring steel arm. At least from there I managed to stop the tractor. Then I had a period of quiet but painful meditation.

It was on such a field that Reg Frith drove his girlfriend for the first time and to my family watching from the side of the field it was a very long drive. The little pick-up kept bobbing up and down over the butts and reans and round and round the field, until eventually it stopped out in the middle of the meadow, some forty-five minutes later. Dad asked Reg why had he not stopped earlier, to which Reg replied with some feeling that Dad hadn't explained how to stop the thing. So he had to keep on driving until it had run out of petrol!

When my uncle Arthur and his bride took over their first farm there was a lot of their pasture fields in butts and reans, in fact it was there that I saw the how effective they were in a thunder storm. My uncle kept a large Irish wolfhound, of which he was very proud — to my young eyes it looked a big ugly dog that, as a breed, had outlived their usefulness. I have no doubt that a few hundred years ago when wolves roamed the Cheshire plain, such a dog could have given a lot of comfort if you were out and about on a dark winter's night. Now for me it seemed just too big and energetic to be of use on any farm. Uncle Arthur claimed it could quickly catch a hare crossing a field with butts and reans, because the hare had to run up and down each butt whereas his wolfhound leapt from butt to butt. Even if the hare went under a gate the dog would go over it with ease.

He made this boast to Dad when we were on a visit there, so with no more ado we were all off with the dog across the fields. In the second one a hare got up some twenty yards in front of us. Sure enough, the hare did have to run up and down each butt and that great leggy dog seemed to catch up with it in seconds. But the hare was wise; at the last moment as the dog's teeth closed on it, it turned sharply left down the bottom of a rean, and the dog at full speed went flying over the top of the next butt. With tail swishing and legs skidding it tried desperately to turn but by the time it had, the hare was at the fence.

It is an amazing thing about hares, in that they will not try to go through a hedge or fence if a dog is close behind them — the hare will run round the field again in an effort to gain a few yards grace. I believe this is because the hare has to slow down to pop through its hole in the hedge. That one had gained those few yards whilst the wolfhound was doing his high-speed turn and had no trouble slipping through the thick hawthorn hedge and away, leaving behind a frustrated dog, an annoyed uncle and a very amused small boy.

It was just after that that the heavens opened. Although hawthorn is about the best bush or tree to shelter under, we still got a soaking as we crouched under one. We saw then just how efficient the butt and rean system was because each one ran like a brook, while, as we walked home, the butts were remarkable firm under our feet.

CHAPTER
THREE

Water Mills

Water mills were an important part of farming operations. Most birds can grind the grain in their gizzard, where it slowly dissolves into digestible food. They can make use of whole corn, but farm animals cannot use grain unless it has been crushed or ground to break the tough outer skin to allow the animal to absorb the nutriments within. There was no mechanical way to crush or grind a farmer's grain on his own farm, so to feed cows, horses or pigs it was necessary to cart the grain to the nearest water mill. There the miller would run the grain through his mill and re-bag it for the farmer to cart home again.

The nearest water mill to Cheadle Farm was Hulme Mill but unfortunately it no longer worked. I never found out why that mill had closed but motor transport was making it possible to send corn to the most efficient and this competition soon closed many of the smaller mills.

Tom Riley lived at the mill which included a small farm on which he kept pigs and cattle. The problem with keeping pigs is that they always seem to attract rats and if there is also a brook through the farmyard then it is even worse. Rats follow a brook like we follow a highway, so if one flows through a farmyard it provides the rats with a main road in and out of the farm. That farmhouse was joined onto the farm buildings which made it difficult, if not impossible, to keep rats out of the farmhouse.

In the days before poisons were available many different methods were used to catch and kill these vermin. Perhaps the most unusual rat catching method came about one morning when Tom Riley's workman George Shaw went into the house to talk to him. Tom who was sitting in the large kitchen, signalled for George to wait outside the door. Suddenly there was a large explosion and George rushed in to find that Tom had shot a large rat, whilst it was sitting in the carved trellis woodwork on top of the grandfather clock!

Tom Riley augmented his income by operating a haulage business, which consisted of two motor lorries, which were used to take farmers' milk into Manchester. Each morning his lorry would call at our farm collecting the fresh milk and leave the empty churns for the next day. He would go on collecting milk from other farmers to make up a full load, then under the direction of the MMB it would be delivered to various dairies in the city. Tom was a very large and strong man and he could crouch down and put his arms round an eighteen gallon milk tankard, which would weigh about two-hundred pounds, and lift it effortlessly onto his lorry. That round daily trip into Manchester and back was usually over by late lunch, so in the afternoons the lorries were free to haul produce for local farmers or businesses. Well, free that is after all the empty milk churns had been unloaded; to be re-loaded again later that same day, ready to be delivered to each farm the next morning.

Tom Riley was blessed with a delightful daughter Rose. She was every farmer's favourite girl in that she could drive those early temperamental motor lorries, handle those very heavy milk tankards and manage to look both happy and feminine whilst doing it all. My strongest recollection of her though was her hands; milk churns were usually washed in caustic soda and Rose had to handle those wet churns both summer and winter. She would be in and out of her lorry, loading full churns and unloading the returned empties. There were no plastic gloves in those days and the wet soda dried out the skin on her hands, and of course in winter the skin cracked. I was only a boy when she showed her hands to me; now some fifty years later, I can can still see those awful open cracks at the base of two fingers on each hand and across one thumb.

Rose's reputation as a driver was legendary. One local man who had joined the Manchester police told how he was on point duty in a dense fog in the heart of the city. It was a real pea-soup fog and drivers were almost all lost. The policeman was trying to bring order to the chaos at a major road junction when Rose drove up in her milk lorry. He stood and stared in amazement as she threaded her way through the thick fog, in and out of the jumble of lost drivers with stationary cars and went on her way untroubled. It was inevitable that Rose was whisked away by a young farmer, much to the disappointment of others. There was even a few grumbles of disapproval from some of the old farmers whose days she had brightened.

Perhaps I should now tell you more about water mills, which I had started to do before I went off chasing those rats! I have based the next few paragraphs on notes compiled by one of William Lea's descendants, Herbert Lea CBE, who compiled them in 1975 when his family celebrated 300 years of continuous trading as millers.

The first record of the Lea family connection with water mills was in 1675 when Thomas de Swettenham granted William Lea the tenancy of a mill that he had built on the brook called "Midge Brook" five miles north west of Congleton. Herbert Lea tells how that first mill at Swettenham included a kiln for drying the grain, which would be converted into flour and oatmeal. As Lord of the Manor, Thomas de Swettenham would have control of the milling there, and this is illustrated in a record of a lease of a farm at nearby Lower Withington:-

"The indenture made on the 26th November, 1742 between Thomas de Swettenham Esq., of the one part and Thomas Norbury of Lower Withington, Yeoman, of the other part, witnesseth that the said Thomas Swettenham, hath granted to farm and to let to the said Thomas Norbury all that messuage situate in the township of lower Withington and the said Thomas Nor-bury covenants that he will grind all his corn at the mill

44

of Thomas Swettenham, . . . and send a sufficient workman with a shovel to assist and help in repairing the breach if any extra-ordanary breach shall happen to the weir or dam at Swettenham Mill Pool."

The Arms of Swettenham of Swettenham depict a shield surmounted by a tree which is being climbed by a lion and diagonally across the shield are depicted three spades. I can only presume that a shovel or spade played some important part in the life of the Swettenham family. On our more humble side "Lea" is the Saxon word for "Meadow". That tenancy agreement shows that the great and the humble combined together to so tie up the tenants that, not only did they have to put all their grain through the landlord's mill, they also had to turn out with a shovel on a stormy wet night if the dam was in danger.

The first Lea millers would have only worked for the landlord. One or two generations later they became tenants, just paying a rent to the landlord. I have not seen a copy of a miller's tenancy agreement; I can only presume that it included some form of royalty paid by the miller to the owner on through-put, because most landlords of that time included a clause tying their tenant farmers to use only their mill.

The Lea family must have had flour dust in their blood because there are records that indicate that different branches of our family ran water mills at Higher Peover, Lower Peover, Somerford Booths, Wistaston, Wybunbury, Sandbach, Brereton — and even that list may be incomplete. What I cannot say for sure is that all those Lea millers originated from the Swettenham Mill Lea family. From the research that I have done I believe that my own family did, and that my branch of the Lea family left the mills and took to full time farming about 1800. It must be remembered that all those water mills would have had a farm attached, to provide keep for the horses needed at the mill, and also a means of a second income for the miller when the mill business was slack.

Herbert Lea tells us about his branch of the Lea family and their proud record of well over 300 years of milling. They still trade from the former water mill at Wheelock where the family business was incorporated in 1926 as "H.J.Lea and Sons Limited, Millers Corn and Seed Merchants". In 1941 "Morning Foods Limited, North Western Mills, Crewe, Oat Millers" was formed to help cover the shortage of oat products during the War. It had the full support of the Ministry of Food, and Philip Lea became the mill manager. He had been a flour miller with the Rank Organisation and had studied cereal chemistry and mill engineering. The manufacture of "Mornflake" flaked oats, oatmeal and other oat products has continued unbroken since then, and I believe that Philip's son John Lea now heads this family-owned company. He also has two sons, so who knows how long this branch of the family will be involved in milling?

Farming is still very dependent on mills but today we have become more remote from them. The ability to haul cattle food long distances coupled with the

46

importation of many feed products means that farmers seldom use their own grain on their own farms. For my father it was just the opposite; in the tight financial straits of the thirties his grain was the cheapest product available. His main worry was how to get it milled and back to the farm as economically as possible. There were five water mills that might have once served our farm but there were only two still working by 1938. The closest was Halford Mill in Tabley but that one was having trouble with the waterwheel and Jim Gough (who comes into my story later on) was called in to repair it. With Halford Mill unreliable, it left only Bate Mill fully operational, on the Peover Eye further up on the border of Over Peover and Lower Withington.

Jack Baxter ran quite a big business from it; at its peak he had two motor lorries and a staff of five or six people. Of course the actual water mill was only a part of his business, because he also sold imported foodstuffs to blend with home-grown grain. These were being used much more in the late 1930s to add protein to the home-grown cereals. The milk market was changing dramatically under the MMB, who were encouraging farmers to increase winter milk production. Cows needed the stimulus of a more sophisticated concentrate ration to milk through the winter to that previously used for the mainly spring calving herds in the pre-MMB low price period.

Bate Mill was the only water mill that I actually saw working. As a small boy I went into it with Dad and was told to stand in one corner whilst he went to find Jack Baxter. The eighteen foot in diameter waterwheel was inside the mill and there was no safety rails or protection, just a kerb to stop spilled grain from falling into the water. I could have easily walked through and into the working waterwheel. As you can imagine, I became fascinated with the workings of the mill and gradually crept closer and closer until I was right by the churning waterwheel. That was where Dad caught me and I got a good shaking for not staying where I was told to! I still regret not being shown through that working mill then, but I fully accept that the only thing that protects country children is discipline. Even today when we have every possible guard in place we must still instill commonsense and responsibility if our children are to live with livestock and machinery. Farming parents have to find a balance between absolute safety, which would entail a high security fence around their garden with the children inside it, or allowing them freedom to experience nature and farming, with all the dangers involved.

The water mill in Lower Peover closed in the late 1930s. It had been run by four generations of the Lea family, and was of course powered by the Peover Eye up stream from Cheadle Farm. Although there is no record of the transactions between my Father and the mill, I am fairly certain that he did trade there because it was only a mile away from our farm, and it was an important trading company within that part of Cheshire. Lower Peover was a large mill in that it had two water wheels, each working independently of the other, but both driven from the same mill pond. The large wheel on the west side was more likely to be used for grain to feed cattle or pigs. The smaller east side wheel with a slower through-put would be used for wheat or oats for human consumption but by no means exclusively.

The difference between milling for cattle or humans was in the degree of grinding the grain; to make bread the wheat would be ground down into a much finer flour than for cattle or pigs. Taffy Williams was the head miller and he lived in one of the Pump Cottages just below the Church. His assistant was Harold Ward and the reputation and success of the mill depended on the skill of these two highly respected craftsmen. When a farmer or smallholder brought grain to the mill they would specify what it was to be used for; if for animal food, whether it was for pigs or cattle, or for poultry, because although fowl could eat whole grain many farmers fed them a hot mash. If the flour was for household use then each farmer's wife would have her own idea as to how fine the flour should be — although Taffy had a reputation for being a bit cantankerous when it came to dealing with some of the more difficult requests.

Lower Peover's Mill had a kiln to dry grain for human use, which must have been an advantage in wet years. On the other hand it was expensive to dry wheat that way so many people relied on oats for their own use. In wet years oats were easier to harvest than wheat and oats could also be used with a slightly higher moisture content, making them a more reliable crop if a farmer was to be sure of feeding his family throughout the winter. They were used as porridge, and in a variety of oat cakes, but sometimes the oatmeal was mixed with wheat flour to make the larger flat bannocks. We had some when on holiday on Orkney recently and they were delicious.

The ability to produce those different grades of flour and crushed grain was dependent on the skill of the miller. Taffy could control the water throughput to slow or quicken the speed of each wheel but more importantly the speed at which he fed the grain to each grindstone. By reducing the rate that grain flowed into the grinding wheel he could produce a much finer flour and of course his skill was in producing the flour or coarse ground cattle food that each customer had ordered. The only concession to hygiene was that flour for human consumption was put into white sacks instead of the normal brown hessian for animals.

The millstones were believed to have come from France and were made from a very hard white stone; not one large stone but nine or ten smaller stones cut to fit into a strong iron hoop to form a wheel. They would gradually wear smooth through continuous use, then the top stone had to be lifted off and both stones had to be re-dressed to rough them up. Taffy often did this skilled job himself but a visiting "journeyman stone dresser" would periodically call and give them expert attention.

Horses were more particular in that they required oats just flattened but not ground down into meal, and particularly containing no dust. To get this ideal horse food, oats need just to be crushed flat without being broken. For this there was a roller wheel that was also driven by the large water wheel, and could be run in addition to the large grinding stone.

With so many different customers having grain ground throughout a day, by closing time there was quite a bit of dust to sweep up. Whose bag would you put it in? The miller couldn't sweep up after each individual lot went through, nor could he put all the sweepings into the last customer's bag particularly if it was for breadmaking. Taffy solved the problem by keeping a few pigs and always carrying a empty sack on his bike handle-bars — well, it was empty when he went to work but coming home it wasn't. Schoolboys used to call after the mill horse team "Miller's horses are always fat", suggesting that the miller creamed a bit out of each sack. If he wanted to, it would be easy to do, because most small farmers would have no means to weigh. When grain had gone through the mill it was much more bulky than whole grain, which meant that the farmer always got more sacks back than he sent to the mill, and he had no way of checking that it had all returned.

No one ever challenged Taffy because he was doing nothing wrong. Had he put the dusty sweepings into someone else's sack there could well have been a complaint. Those sweepings mixed with water made good pig food! Taffy lived at Pump Cottage within a few yards of the graveyard and he had a reputation for keeping a good strain of pigs. He also kept a boar for hire and many local farmers and cottagers would bring their sow to be served by it. Mating a pig is a completely different thing than a cow. The bull has one quick jump and the job is done. A boar on the other hand mounts the sow and then settles there for a more relaxed affair. In fact if you were waiting to take your sow home again after she had been served, there would be time to discuss the weather, how good the harvest had been, a few comments about the government and have a cup of tea before the old boar had blinked for the last time. Those old pig-men used to say that every time the boar blinked it was another piglet. I am sure that if you saw a boar mating you would realise with some surprise just where the term originated from. If you remember that when you next call someone an "old boar", you too may blink at the thought.

The Peover Eye is often thought of as a placid little brook but like most water courses, a heavy storm can prove it otherwise. In 1872 there was very heavy rain across Mid-Cheshire. Near the source of the brook below Macclesfield, about five inches fell in a few hours. Henbury Pool overflowed and as the flood travelled down stream it gathered momentum. At Chelford where the two streams from Siddington and Henbury pass under the A535 before joining to form the Peover Eye, both those bridges were washed away. Bate Mill lies about two miles down stream and there the flood washed the pigs out of their sties. When the water rose at Lower Peover, Willy Lea's father struggled to rescue the corn from the ground floor of the mill, but the water rose so quickly that he almost lost his life in the effort. I have no knowledge of what happened to the livestock at that mill, but in the same storm the rain was so heavy that the nearby Bradshaw Brook also flooded. It rose so high that the flood water was up to the cows' udders whilst they stood tied in their stalls at Bradshaw Brook Farm.

Willy Lea and his wife Ellen took over the mill in 1903, just three years after the new house had been built for them at the mill. They were the third generation of the Lea family to run the mill. Their son Edgar was to follow on the tradition but the First World War took him away for some years to fight bravely in far off lands. He was promoted to the rank of captain and was highly respected by the local people. Before the War he had been engaged to a local girl but somewhere in his travels he met a London beauty. Her home was in Romford in Essex and the Lea family had a long journey to attend Edgar's wedding. I have no record of what happened to the local girl but Edgar's new bride Kate was an exceptional beauty. Even today, some seventy years later, people who saw her still remember how, when she walked down the street in Knutsford, her looks were so strikingly attractive that all heads turned; both male and female would look in stunned admiration.

Willy developed what appears to have been multiple sclerosis although there was no diagnoses at that time. There was, though, for his daughter Vivian who developed the illness early in her own life and was in a nursing home in London for many years before she died. Two other daughters Amy and Janet helped to run the business. They were also involved in the work on the farm where about ten cows were kept and their calves reared, as well as the heavy horses needed to cart grain and cattle food to and from the mill. Old records of Lower Peover show that the Leas rented additional land, making their farming business much larger than the present mill site.

The young calves, that the two girls reared, were tethered in summer on the meadow next to the mill pond and one was tied to a cherry tree; somehow it managed to get free and in its excitement it jumped into the mill pond. Cattle can swim but often they don't know it and are afraid. This one managed to splash on to a shallow spot behind some bushes that overhung the pool and stayed there. It stood with head and shoulders well above the water but to get out it would have had to swim through deeper water, and of course it was too afraid to do that, so Taffy was called from the mill to help in the rescue. Taffy was renowned for his ability to swear, but to save the girls embarrassment he swore in Welsh. He swore profusely whilst he splashed about trying to get a rope around what was a strong calf. Eventually he did get the rope round its neck and between him and the girls they managed to pull it free. But it was a toss-up who was most wet, Taffy or the calf.

The Lower Peover water wheels were called overshot wheels, the type usually seen restored today. For that type of wheel the water has to be damned high enough to flow over the top of the wheel where it hits the paddles, called stops — the spokes are called starts — at the top of their cycle. They were made so that they held the water when it flowed onto them and it was the weight of water rather than the flow that turned the wheel round.

A different type were called pelting wheels and were possible the earliest type of water wheel. They were usually smaller in diameter, with the water flowing so that it struck the bottom of the wheel, just like a paddle steamer only in reverse, the flow of water hitting the paddles which turned the mill wheel. I believe that it was neither as efficient or powerful as the overshot type and most of them had gone out of use before the twentieth century. As well as the overshot and undershot wheels there were pitch-back wheels (overshot wheels working in the opposite direction) and breast wheels. There may have been many other kinds of water power through the last few thousand years. Some historians claim that the Romans introduced the first water mills to this country. But we know that we were farming some two thousand years or more before the Romans came, and on some of the Scottish Islands there is ample evidence to show that we were quite good stonemasons then, so I would not be surprised to learn that the water mill was in use here before Roman times.

I know of nine different recent mill sites on the Peover Eye and its tributaries but I am sure there were many more mills through history. Nearly all of the nine would have been designed and made differently, each site with its individual terrain to design around and of course each builder his own idea of the best design. Each mill had its own arrangement of weirs, hatches, sluices, races, leats or bypass channels, but in all of them the water went to the wheel via the mill-race and left it along the tail-race.

The breast-wheel was the name given to more than one type of wheel, but in each case the water hit the wheel at breast height. Perhaps the smallest and simplest of those mill wheels was one where the water struck a horizontal wheel, almost like a turn-stile, needing a much smaller building and less water to drive it. The paddles were no more than flat boards protruding from a wooden hub, the hub upright and the paddles out at right angles from four sides. The water came out of a small spout to hit them side on with speed. Remarkably there is one still in working order on Orkney, where it is called a "click mill". Each paddle is just over a foot in length, and butted into a short oak stump also of about a foot in diameter, so the total width of the water wheel is only about three to four feet. The spindle goes straight up through the water wheel and into the grinding wheel in the mill directly above, with no cogs or gears or belts. The "click" was caused by an oak peg set into the grinding wheel which at every cycle tripped a lever to release a small amount of grain to give a continuous flow through the mill. A remarkably simple set up, but its output would be very small, perhaps only grinding enough grain for one or two very small farms.

I believe that there were many more water mills than the ones we know of today. The action of the wheel and machinery created a constant vibration that shook the most robust buildings, and this meant that the mill house was often pulled down and rebuilt, usually on the same spot but with refinements as each generation improved in knowledge and experience. I am also sure that the very early water mills would have been much smaller, providing for fewer people, in isolated localities. Those mills could have been situated on very small brooks where there was less danger from severe flooding. A small brook took longer to refill the mill pond, and could only drive a small wheel, which would in turn mean a low output. They were perhaps built from our long lasting oak, with no more than a stone base and the grinding stones — which could be moved and used elsewhere — so there would be no trace today other than perhaps a hint of the remains of a damn.

Lower Peover mill could direct the full flow of the stream into the mill pond and on through the water wheels. There were even extra weirs, up stream, to hold more water back, and these could be released when the mill pond was empty and the stream was low in dry weather. The mill dam and pool are still in place, as is the dam across the brook which diverts the flow into the mill pool. The footpath from the church crosses the brook over that dam, which is known as Paddles Bridge. The water doesn't flow over the top of the dam but out through two large pipes. When the mill was working there were two large, almost cricket bat-shaped paddles that could be lowered independently to close off one or both of the large outlet pipes to divert the water into the mill pool.

The need to conserve enough water to drive the mill throughout a full day's work was paramount to any other job. At lunch time Willy Lea would ring a large brass bell and Taffy would rush to close the two sluice gates that controlled the flow from the mill pond to each wheel and the "mill would grind to a halt" (yes, that is where the saying came from). After lunch the bell would ring to open the sluice gates to "start the wheels turning". Any farmer who was waiting at the mill whilst his grain was being ground would have joined the family and staff for the meal. It was a tradition of the mill that anyone was welcome and if a horseman had left home early in the morning to bring a load of grain to the mill, the girls would cook a breakfast for him whilst Taffy put his corn "through the mill" (another saying that as been handed down to us).

Before the motor waggon, the mill ran two horsedrawn delivery vehicles. One, driven by Billy Cross, was a small shandrey, for carrying a few sacks to the smaller customers, and between loads Billy would help out in the mill. The teamsman was Tom Cragg who lived at Foxcovert Cottage. He drove a team of heavy horses who pulled the heavy four-wheeled lorry. The team consisted of one shire in the shafts, plus a chain horse in front, but a second chain horse could be added. The cobbled drive slopes down to the mill, which meant that the horses had to start their journey up bank, which they did not like. Those old cart horses would be aware of each sack as it was dropped onto their lorry, knowing that they would have to pull them all up that steep incline. You can imagine them standing quietly in the shafts thinking "Damn him, he is putting another one on and he expects me to pull that lot up that hill!" So sometimes they would refuse to start. The problem was overcome by making a second drive out alongside the brook onto Mill Lane. The result, a more gentle incline which suited the horses much better. The strange thing was that when the horses come to the steeper incline later in their journey, they took it in their stride.

In our time at Cheadle Farm the mill team of horses was replaced by an Albion motor lorry, Tom Cragg's pride and joy which he serviced and maintained faithfully. Tom drove it regularly to Liverpool Docks to collect imported foodstuffs, particularly the large grained whole maize which was ground through the mill and sold to farmers for £4 per ton as "Indy meal".

Willy Lea became very handicapped with MS to the point where his family and staff used to carry him out into the mill yard so that he could watch the mill work and chat to the many visitors. There were many callers through the length of a day, some with perhaps only one sack of grain for their own bread making; others negotiating the sale of surplus grain or buying imported proteins to enrich their home produced grain. As Willy became more handicapped the bell was used by Mrs Lea to summon Edgar, or one of the staff from the mill, when she needed help to lift his father.

Edgar Lea's role was that of travelling salesman. After he came home from the War he cycled round his farmer customers, but in later years he used a small car. On his travels within Mid-Cheshire he sold animal feeds and various seeds and also bought surplus grain from farmers. That grain was sold either through the mill feeds or on to other feed merchants further away.

CHAPTER
FOUR

A Glimpse Further Back

Events makes us what we are, not just those within our own lives but back into the lives of our parents and even beyond them. Farmers in particular benefit (or suffer) from the inheritance of knowledge; but it is not just knowledge, more a genetic feel for both the countryside and a need to be close to it.

In past times there wasn't the means to develop different careers, which made some farmers feel trapped and resentful. Now, with modern education, new opportunities have opened up that may appear both more rewarding and less demanding in terms of time and intrusion into family life, and many farming children are turning away from their parents' way of life. Most of them have grown up under the influence of parents who accept the demands of seasonal work, and the need to look after a calving cow before the pleasure of a evening out. Although those young people may have rejected their parents' way of life as too demanding, they often take their parents' commitment into their own sphere of work and are successful because of it.

I have often noticed, though, how many of those who have turned their back on farming for their career, return again to it later in life. It may be full time or just a few acres as a hobby. Sometimes it is the grandchildren who come back to farming, but whichever, I believe that it is a motivation within them that is stronger than mere logic.

My farming friends are not going to appreciate the following illustrations but I would like to use them to enlarge on my ideas about genetics. Throughout most of my farming years I always had two dogs, sometimes more, but if possible at least one labrador and one sheepdog have shared my life. Each in their completely different ways helped considerably to make things easier for me. A young and somewhat tactless reporter wrote a piece about me some twenty years ago. In it he said that, "*He farms his farm with his two dogs and his wife Celia*". Needless to say, "*His wife Celia*" was not too chuffed with that order of merit. The point I want to make is that those two breeds of dogs have the same DNA, and are scientifically one species but by careful selection man has created completely different instincts and responses to circumstances.

Looking round livestock is a daily routine, in fact for me it has always been one of the most enjoyable parts of my farming life. I have always carried a set of field glasses in my Landrover and invariably I would see something of interest besides looking at the livestock. On this occasion it was the livestock themselves that

61

took my interest. In one field there was a group of about thirty large bullocks, and some of them had been reaching through the brookside fence and snapped off three fence posts. In fact one big black beast was just going through the broken fence but turned back when I shouted. Had I gone home for fencing equipment and help, the bullocks would have been through the fence before I could have got back. Once through they would have trampled down my neighbour's mowing grass — and I have always tried hard to not to upset my neighbours. So my only option was to move those bullocks quickly onto another field.

I had just lost Robbie my faithful collie, who had worked into his fifteenth year and then faded quickly away. Drake the labrador was always game to join in anything I was doing — he would bark on command and often helped to drive the dairy cows — but bullocks were in a different league. When Drake barked behind a dairy cow lazing in the field, it would quickly head for home to be milked. When he barked behind a bullock that wanted to go into the neighbour's mowing, it still headed for the mowing, only much more quickly, and Drake hadn't the skill to turn it in the other direction. After a lot of stick waving and shouting I managed to turn them away from the broken fence, but it was only when I put Drake back into the Landrover, and used the vehicle as a dog, dashing about at speed, that I, in the end, managed to get them all into the next field. After that episode I soon went out to buy a replacement driving dog!

62

On the other hand every collie dog that I have owned has enjoyed hunting and shooting but with no thought of cooperation other than to hunt on command. One evening early in my farming life I had taken my collie down to the far end of the farm to move some heifers on to a fresh field. The rabbits had been living up to their reputation, so I had taken the shotgun intending to shoot a few on the way home. I was on the tractor in the days before tractor cabs which made it easy to carry the shotgun across my knees. To raise the gun and shoot from a sitting position on the tractor, I found better than stalking them on foot. I shot two, each time stepping down off the tractor to pick them up myself.

I then shot one on the opposite bank of a deep sided brook and sent my collie to retrieve it. Now this was a well-controlled dog who would move to the left or the right, go back or come forward, sit down or stand up, all on command. He proved how obedient he was by jumping the brook when told to, and he went straight to the rabbit, but obedience stopped there! He had what is best described as a confusion of instincts, which he solved by sitting down and eating the rabbit despite every thing I said (well, "said" gives the wrong impression because by the time he had finished I was quite red in the face). Both of those were dogs that I was proud to own, and both wanted to please, but in the end they responded to the natural forces with in them.

I know we are above animals in that we have the ability to reason, but the point I am trying to make is that those of us who have come from many generations, if not thousands of years, of farming stock have an in-built relationship with the countryside which is hard to rationalise. Although it is simple to decide that we should live and work elsewhere, the instinct is not easily shed even after one or two generations away from the country life.

The Lea family seem to have been involved with farming as far back as I can trace, in as much that the water mills were always part of a farm. Because of this I thought you might like a brief look at what farming was like in Mid-Cheshire, and the kind of life my ancestors enjoyed, both two centuries and one century before my parents started farming. The experiences of our forebears helped to shape my parents' outlook on life and in turn my own.

Around 1750 farms were often let on a lease for three lives. The lives had to be named so a farmer could name himself and two others, usually his children which gave him in effect a tenancy for two generations. He would have to pay an initial "fine" of about £110 or even more if it were a larger farm and then a small rent of £8 to £10 per year. He or his heirs would be charged a "herriot" on the death of any of the named people in the lease. This second "herriot" or "fine" was much smaller than the first one. In the past it had been the farmer's best beast, but by the mid-eighteenth century it was a sum of money usually, about £3 to £5. To put it all in perspective the initial fine was equal at that time to the total value of about fifty cows. When you remember that the farmer we are describing would have about six cows on perhaps a fifty acre farm (size of farms were seldom recorded at that time), £110 was a massive "ingoing" to pay.

The landlord's control over his tenants went much further into their lives than now. On top of the rent most tenants had to do "boon work", a set number of days of free work done for the landlord on his estate. Each boon had a value and the landlord had the option to charge if the work wasn't done i.e. 1 day's ploughing or 2/6; 1 day's harrowing or 2/-. At Nether Peover the tenants had to use the landlord's watermill at Tabley because he didn't own the one at Lower Peover, which for many was a much longer journey.

An Inventory

A true and perfect inventory of all the goods Catells and Chattells, moveables and unmoveables of George Jackson of Nether Peover in the countie of Chester, yoman who departed this life the second day of October A.D. 1641 and were praised by Thomas Henshall, Thomas Allen, Peter Jackson and Thomas Burgess the second day of November of the same year.

	£	s.	d.
For six kyne	14.	0.	0.
for six younge beasts	11.	0.	0.
for two calves	1.	10.	0.
for two mares and two horses	10.	0.	0.
for two colts	4.	0.	0.
for three swine	3.	0.	0.
for barley	17.	0.	0.
for oates pease and beans	13.	0.	0.
for hey	12.	0.	0.

	£	s.	d.
for strawe		5.	0.
for a ladder, two gates, a carts blades, and a pole to make a cart of		18.	8.
for five paire of chaines, seaven paire of hames, five collars, one cart saddle, two cart ropes with other ropes	1.	4.	0.
for an axe, a hatchett, foure pikells, two shovells, two bills, one forke, three iron wedges and a worthing hook		8.	6.
for a corne cart, two old paire of wheeles, a muck cart, a payre of draughts, an axeltree, three ploughs, and two harrows	2.	5.	0.
for towe braked and unbraked	2.	18.	0.
for a sett of spokes, a corne shovell, a whole measure, a halfe measure, a peck, a hetchow, six sives, an old sith, a hey hooke, three yarwingle stockes, five sackes, a poke, two winnowsheets and a cart sheete	1.	2.	1.
for foure old gooses and eighteen young ones		16.	0.
for a grindle stone, two cheesepresses, two swine troughs, a kneading			
trough and a mooding board		13.	4.
for cannell, turves and wood	1.	2.	0.
for foure hens and two cockes		2.	0.
for hempe seed, an old coffer and a turnell		10.	0.
for six leaves, groates, meal, malt, old bacon, a hundred of cheese and butter	2.	6.	0.
for two boards, two sawes, plough irons and old iron		18.	10.
for a payre of bedstockes, a chaff bed, an old cadowe, an old bolster and five reeles and yarnestaves		6.	0.

	£	s.	d.
for foure paire of flaxen sheets, seaven paire of round sheets, a dozen of napkins and other naprie ware	3.	13.	4.
for bolsters, feather beds, pillows, two blanketts, a chaffe bed and three chaffe bolsters	5.	3.	0.
for a bed, a table and a lyvery cupboard	1.	15.	0.
for a bed, a chest, a deske, a table, two blanketts and a bedhilling	3.	10.	0.
for a paire of bedstockes, two chaffe beds, a coverlett, a blanket and a bolster		19.	4.
for a spinning wheele, an old ark, a lyttle ark and a planke		6.	0.
for a coverlett, two blanketts, two bolsters and a chaffe bed	1.	0.	0.
for a chaffe bed, a bolster, two coverletts, a blanket and the bedstockes		10.	0.
for a cupboard, a table and a forme, and a little falling board	1.	14.	4.
for chayres, stooles and cushions		8.	0.
for treen ware and earthen ware	3.	12.	6.
for three slippings of yarn		1.	6.
for pewter	2.	12.	0.
for pott brasse	3.	0.	0.
for panne brasse	3.	0.	0.
for three spitts, a dreeping panne, a grate, cobards, pottrackes, potthookes, fyre shovells, tongs, grid iron, bellowes and a cleever	1.	0.	0.
for a looking glass, a salt coffer, salt pipe and smoothing iron		3.	6.
for a dishboard and a water board		12.	6.

	£	s.	d.
for a broken grass in Tabley ground	5.	0.	0.
for his tack of Tabley ground	60.	0.	0.
owing by Mr Smallwood clerke	2.	0.	0.
owing by Robert Worrall of Northwich upon bond	2.	19.	0.
for his wearing apparrell	7.	0.	0.
Total	209.	12.	5.

In 1737 the Cholmondleys of Holford sold their estate at Little (Lower) Peover to Sir Francis Leicester of Tabley and all the tenants on the Tabley Estate had to join the Cheshire Cavalry. When needed in a time of war or for training, each farmer of below fifty acres had to provide a man or a horse, those above fifty acres had to provide both, and each June they had to take part in two week's training at Chester. This was right in their hay harvest, perhaps the only two weeks of good haymaking sunshine of the summer and they were prancing about in Chester miles away from their hayfields! They didn't like this one bit and appealed for a reduction in rent. To the relief of everyone, the landlord abolished the cavalry instead! At this stage the Leicesters probably became owners of the Lower Peover mill and, in all, life must have improved considerably for all concerned.

The landlord still had control of the tenants in as much that they still had to do the boon work, and also to provide him with one cock for cock-fighting, or a cheese or capon, and some farmers had to keep a dog for the landlord's use. The tenant also had to plant twenty young trees every seven years and allow the landlord to plant about a hundred. The tenant was not allowed to cut timber without permission and then only for repairs known as "houseboot", "cartboot" and "plowboot". There was, though, the right of "turbary", that is the right to cut turves and peat from certain mosses that the landlord owned, and that peat would be their main burning fuel.

All manure generated had to be returned to that land and they had to dig and spread marl. There were many more petty restrictions on what could be grown and where, on how much land could be ploughed each year, and the need to replace tillage with good grass seed and clover. The tenants were not allowed to "sublet or to receive, harbour or entertain any inmates in the said dwelling house". Nor could they take game or fish, or keep anything that could be used for that purpose.

With no cavalry training and the use of the nearest watermill, those independent-minded farmers had more time to get on with their busy lives. From wills and inventories, it is obvious that in those days farming really was hard work. They grew oats, barley and wheat, and also hemp, from which they made sacks and tow, a coarse fibre. They nearly all had linen sheets and napkins woven from homegrown flax; and they grew potatoes, peas, beans, and vetches, and some kept bees.

The inventories of these farmers, known as yeomen or husbandmen, were very varied but usually included about six kyne (cows), six young heifers (or stirks) and some calves. These were not small farmers, and the move from oxen to horses was apparent from the fact that three horses and two or three colts, plus their gear, were in most inventories. About eight sheep, plus a smaller number of swine, hens, ducks and geese, made the list of crops and livestock into the illustration of a really mixed farm.

A spinning wheel and a cheese press were in almost every will or inventory, because both were used to make saleable items. Although it would appear from the list above that they were very self sufficient in both food and clothing, there was still a need for real money and cheese was the main revenue earner of that time. To illustrate this, some inventories showed that the cheese in hand could be almost as much in value as the six cows, and of course it would both keep and be easy to transport.

It would be amiss not to mention the most revolutionary thing to happen in the countryside at that time. It was of course the Enclosures Act. It changed the shape of rural England. Prior to it, each farmer or villager had several strips of land which were not fenced or even next to each other, so he often had to travel long distances between them. There were also large areas of common land attached to each village where most of the livestock grazed.

The Enclosures Act was to rationalise this nonsense and it was achieved by appointing two commissioners who came to the village and took all the land in hand to redistribute it fairly. Like most good intentions this scheme ended in rough justice for some; fair seemed to mean fairly good for the larger farmer and landowner and fairly bad for the small farmer and cottager. Prior to this the small farmer made his living by working as a casual labourer through the busy times of the year for his larger neighbours. When there was no work to be had with them, he could work at home and to a degree live off the produce of his few small strips of land. And of course he relied almost completely on the open commons to provide grazing for his beasts.

With only between five and six million people in the country, you would have thought that there would be enough land to go round, but the reality was quite different. After the Enclosures had taken place, most of the land had been allotted to the nearest holding but because both the cottager and many smaller farmers lived in the village their houses were quite close together. It was not possible to allot much land where houses were almost side by side, so those who lived in them lost out on the redistribution of the strips. In addition they also lost their right to graze the commons, which were fenced and made part of much larger farms. Although some small farmers still managed to make a living from their farms with some additional outside work, it was the end of a way of life for many part-time farmers. It would appear that all this had taken place in Lower Peover early in the eighteenth century because the tenancy agreements that I have used as examples place so much importance on the need to plant trees in hedgerows. These were new hedgerows to enclose the new fields created by the Enclosures Act and the countryside took on a new vista.

What is noticeable from Lower Peover village history, is that at least four relatively large sums of money were given in the first half of that century to form different charities to help feed the poor. My belief is that many village people were severely impoverished by the loss of both their most productive strips and the right to graze the common land.

It was also in that century that the canals were dug. Although none went through the Peover area, the nearest being at Middlewich and Northwich, they provided transport for both the provisions and produce relating to agriculture. The need to get to the canal wharfs, plus the greater reliance on the shire horse to haul large loads across country, brought about the end of many of the old packhorse routes. In their place that century saw the creation of new roads, but they were more winding than the old packhorse roads because they needed to follow more gentle contours and firm ground.

If we jump another hundred years to the first half of the nineteenth century we find that the population of the Country had risen to over seven million people. Cheese was still the major commodity in Cheshire farming and Peover was still very much a mixed farming area but the dairy cow was at the centre of most farming operations. On the westerly fringe, though, the soil was of a more heavy clay, and in those parts dairy herds had increased in size until a sixty-cow herd was not uncommon and there was even a very occasional one hundred-cow herd. The milk from those herds in the nineteenth century was used almost completely for cheese making.

Although Cheshire Cheese had a nationwide reputation it was amazing that there was no standard procedure, each farmer's wife or cheese maker using their own recipe; and yet the results gave a similar type of cheese. The Gazetteer and Directory of Cheshire published in 1860 tells us. "There exists no foundation for an attempt at uniformity. The degree of heat at the setting of the milk together is never measured, the quantity of steep is guessed at, and the quality not exactly known; the quantity of salt necessary is undefined, and the sweating of the cheese is accidental." It is no wonder that there was some variation in the end product, with some farms earning the highest reputation, and of course the better price, whilst others were only second best.

One of my father's friends was the cheese factor Gwin Williams from Holmes Chapel, who had been taught by his father and made his reputation in the early twentieth century by being able to select the best of the County's cheese. Two rules I remember him saying he used, apart from his knowledge of which farm could produce the best cheese. Firstly, always try to choose cheese made from September grass milk. Having chosen what he thought was the best cheese from the best farm, he would then press his thumb into it; if the cheese didn't spring back he rejected it. If it passed those two tests he would go on to "iron" it, that is to take a taste from the centre.

The difference between spring and autumn cheese was created by the fact that the cheese farms all had spring calving herds, living outside all the year round and calving in a two month period from late March through to early May. This was to make the best use of the highly productive early summer grass. On this system cows would give the most milk in May and June then production would fall through July with perhaps a second much smaller flush towards September, but they would all be dry before Christmas. By September, milk production had fallen so much that milk would have to be saved for up to four weeks before there was enough to make a vat of cheese; and this gave the best cheese. The milk was stored in large stone vats — there is one in my farmyard which is over a cubic yard in size. Although it is skilfully hollowed out it still must weigh well over half a ton when empty. I can only presume that the thick stone walls of the vat remained cold which would help the milk to keep longer.

Those cheese producing farmers prayed for a wet grass-growing summer. The fact that it was difficult to make good hay in that type of a year was not a problem, because poor quality hay would do to feed their dry cows through the winter. Their cows were quite small compared to today's cows, and living out side all the year round, never got very fat. The stocking rate was anywhere between two and three acres per cow and the production from each cow was only about 250 lbs of cheese per year. Today we expect a cow to produce at least 1000 lbs of cheese, with some herds averaging over 1400lbs from each cow a year, and that from no more than one acre of grass. Around 1850 it is thought that there was about 95,000 cows in Cheshire producing about 10,000 tons of cheese each year. At a cheese fair held in Crewe on November 29th 1849 over 400 tons of cheese was on display and most of it sold at prices between 40 shillings and 50 shillings per cwt (£40 to £50 per ton).

Tasting cheese was important not just to confirm the quality of each farmer's cheese, but also because there was a need to check for unpleasant taints. What the cows had eaten could be tasted in the cheese; unbelievable as it may sound, the expert cheesemaker could tell, just by tasting, that a field needed dressing with marl. The dictionary says that marl is a mixture of clay and lime. I can't tell the difference between clay and marl, but even ordinary clay will sweeten grass. Those who have dug a drain through a pasture field will have noticed how cattle graze closer to the ground where the clay has lain on the grass, so the effect of marl would have been more marked. We now use lime to achieve the same effect; it not only sweetens the grass but encourages the more productive grasses to grow, as I am sure marl did.

You may think that the best cheese came from beautiful old wild flower meadows. Not necessarily so — even the humble buttercup, if it was too prevalent in the sward, could taint the cheese and some other wildflowers could cause a taint in small numbers. When a taint or unpleasant flavour was discovered the cheesemaker would often be able to guess by the taste and the time of year what had caused it. If it was a wild

75

plant then he would have his large staff walking in a line (like policemen searching the scene of a crime) across his pasture fields or even on their knees if need be, searching for the offensive weeds.

There was an old Cheshire saying, "I never saw a poor cheese maker". It seemed to be true, yet they went a long way through the year without any income — it was usual for them to sell no cheese before September when the bulk of the early summer cheese would be marketed. Often by Christmas most of the cheese had been sold off the farm. The cheese would have stood in a press for a few days to reduce the liquid content and then been carried up into the attic cheese room. The cheeses were stood, one high, on tiers of shelves in a dry but airy room, and had to be turned every day. If a cheese had been made from milk that was too high in butterfat, it would start to sweat in hot weather as the heat melted the butterfat in the cheese. Although that cheese was rejected for keeping quality, it was delicious for cooking and would be used by the family. On the other hand if the milk was too low in butterfat (or from skimmed milk), that cheese would be pale and tasteless.

Most of those outdoor herds of cows were also milked out of doors and in all weathers. The cows would come into the farmyard at milking time and the milkers would often milk them wherever the cows stood. To look after and milk about sixty cows would need in the low teens of people, some perhaps the farmworkers' wives, just helping at milking time. As I have told you earlier, many were young people of both sexes who "lived in", so there would a lot of banter and humour to help the hard work go down.

Dad loved to tell a story about one of his new dairy maids at Cheadle Farm — we are though jumping forward about 50 years and by that time of course the cows were milked inside the shippens. The new girl had to learn to milk so Dad gave her a demonstration of where to sit, where to lean her head and how to squeeze the milk out without getting a kick from the cow. He then sat her on her stool by a quiet, easily-milked cow and left her to milk it. The other milkers were spaced out along the shippen, each on a stool with head pressed against their cows flank. That helped to keep the cows still, but it meant that the milkers could not see much of what was going on elsewhere along the shippen. There was just the sound of milk squirting into buckets and Dad was engrossed in the cow that he was milking.

When the new girl had finished her cow she asked one of the men which should she milk next. Those were the days of stocky roan coloured shorthorn cows and to her inexprienced eye a more stocky roan coloured bull would look much like a cow. After milking his cow, Dad got up off his stool to find that the timid young girl was sitting tight by the side of the bull, her head pressed tightly into his flank right in front of his back leg, just as she had been taught. As she felt around the bull's well endowed scrotum with both hands, she was saying "I can't find any paps". The men were falling of their stools with laughter.

For a young girl or boy coming straight from school, milking was no easy task. Although they could sit down to milk, it took years to build up the strength in their hands. At first they would be given a couple of easy cows to milk and then gradually they would be able to milk another but it could take two or three years to build up the strength to milk five or six cows at a session. Even the most experienced milkers would not expect to milk more than six cows at each milking. It was a matter of skill, strength and stamina, but once their hands became tired, no amount of determination could make those hands milk another cow until they had a few hours rest.

Milking technique was a debateable thing. As children we were taught to squeeze and not to pull. By gripping the teat with all our fingers we could then squeeze the top index finger, then the next one, and the next in turn, creating a ripple effect down the teat. As we released one hand we would squeeze the other using very little pull, but it was difficult if the cow's teats were short. When a man's hands were too broad or the teat too short, he would then have to use thumb and finger to squeeze and pull down with one movement, but cows didn't like that method as much as the other.

Cows would soon get used to a milker's style so with a larger herds like Dad's it was important that anyone could milk any cow. He found that if he let his milkers choose which cows they milked, the cows became more choosy than the staff. Then when a milker was off for the weekend or ill or whatever, the cows that person usually milked could make it very difficult for anyone else to milk them. It wasn't just a matter of kicking, if a cow is not happy she will hold her milk back and make it very hard to milk her. Even when we children were learning to milk, Dad would only let us milk the easy cows a few times, then we had to mix in on others. A child or woman's hand is smaller than a man's and they could use the ripple method to milk the cows with smaller teats much more easily than a man.

The trains came thundering across the Cheshire plain at about 20 miles per hour, and by 1849 the links into Manchester and Liverpool were complete. This added another means of transport for farm produce; arable farmers could now grow perishable crops for the Manchester market. This developed new outlets and brought new wealth into the County. One particular crop gained favour; from the Peover's through to Knutsford and onto Warrington, the soil and climate was favourable for growing early potatoes. Today the area still produces the best flavoured early potatoes in the Country. Those early potatoes were, and still are, harvested in June and July but they need to be eaten fresh because they will only keep a few days after lifting. On a good year early potatoes added considerably to the finances of the late nineteenth century farmers. There was still a wide range of cereals, vegetable and other potato crops grown on those farms so it remained a very mixed farming area. Crop rotation had been developing for over 100 years, and rotations of four to seven years were used by Cheshire farmers to suit their particular farm.

The railway brought the early morning milk train and many farmers gave up cheesemaking to supply the Manchester fresh milk market. The better cheesemakers continued with their trade, but in the latter part of the century even their herds were housed inside in winter. I have looked around many farms in Cheshire and the bulk of the old Cheshire brick farm buildings, (mostly built to house dairy cows) were built around 1850 to 1880. This massive investment in farm buildings shows there must have been considerable prosperity in agriculture at that time. Those lovely brick buildings have served farmers for 100 years or more, and have only become out-dated with the introduction of loose housing and cubicle systems in recent years.

The early morning milk train brought the decline to another kind of farmer: the city cowkeepers who housed their cows within Manchester and Liverpool. There were usually eight to ten cows in a herd and they were often housed in cellars and kept tied up all day and every day. The Cheshire cheesemakers were part of the equation because they only kept their outside calving cows for two or three lactations and then sold them newly calved either at the local town fairs or to cattle dealers. It was a well thought-out policy because a cow's milk falls in both butterfat and protein after the second lactation and through subsequent lactations. Cheesemakers needed the best quality milk so it was better to sell the cow to someone where quality was not so important, and the city cowkeeper was a ready customer for the cheesemakers' old cows.

There were still city cowkeepers operating at the start of the 1939 War, so I have been able to get a fair idea of their way of life. It wasn't much of a life for the old cows they kept. Not only were they tied up all the time, they never saw green grass or met the bull. They were fed on hay and concentrates bought in from merchants, and not being put to the bull they would milk longer than an in-calf cow and would also get fat whilst they were milking. When at last their milk production fell to the point of becoming uneconomic, the cows would take their first walk for about a year, but only around the corner to the nearest butcher who slaughtered and sold them through his shop. In those days there was no trade in prime young beef as there is now — the beef bought in the city butcher's shop was mostly from those aged dairy cows.

The city cowkeeper would get up about 4.30a.m. to milk and then deliver that milk fresh to his customers. He would then return to attend to his cows' needs, have lunch and go to bed until afternoon milking time when he repeated the process. Before the War, milk was 3d per pint and was delivered twice each day. A merchant's representative told me that he could only do business with them in that brief hour or two between their return from delivering milk and going to bed after lunch. On their milk round they would also sell eggs at a shilling per dozen, but in spring, when there was an over-supply, many customers insisted on having thirteen to the dozen. There was no artificial lighting in those days to stimulate the hens to lay in winter, so it meant that there was always a shortage in the dark months of the year.

At Cheadle Farm my mother preserved our eggs in something called "waterglass". It was in fact mixed with water and each spring as children in our turn we spent hours cleaning (but not washing) eggs, placing them in buckets full of the stuff to keep for use through the following winter. Washing was believed to allow bacteria to enter the shells so we didn't preserve very dirty eggs and only wiped with a damp cloth the less dirty ones. Only eggs that were more than 24 hours old but less than four days could be used and when we placed them in the waterglass each egg had to be point down to keep the yoke central. Eggs preserved this way were only good for cooking and could not be boiled or fried.

Through the later part of the nineteenth century farmers had been practising rotational cropping, but only on their arable land and what grassland came into that rotation was mostly short term grassland sown specifically to grow hay. Much of the pasture land had not been ploughed for generations and many older farmers thought it would be sacrilege to put the plough into them. Dad had no such inhibitions. The argument in favour of the old pastures was based on the fact that they were tough and did not tread up by cattle in wet weather. Dad believed that new strains of grass could out-produce the old pastures, and anyway cows were now housed through the winter months so there was much less damage by cows' feet. Father had also realised that there was a terrific store of fertility locked away in those old turfs. By ploughing them he could release that energy to produce much higher crops of potatoes, which he could then follow with a crop of wheat.

Not only did he plough his old pastures in turn but he introduced a six or seven year rotation based on potatoes, wheat, oats, to be followed by a three or four year grass lay. The grass lay had muck spread on it each winter so that when it was eventually ploughed at the beginning of the next rotation, it was nearly as fertile as the original old turf. Farmers in the area thought of him as a revolutionary; some admired him, others loved to see him come unstuck — and in farming it isn't hard to do that. One of Dad's little embarrassments was caused by his determination to plough every possible furrow up each hedge, ditch or brook side.

After leaving school Harry Davies had in fact worked full time for two years for my two uncles. His younger brother Eric took his place there and Harry came to work for Dad. Although he was only just sixteen he already had a life time of experience with horses and by his seventeenth birthday he was a very capable waggoner. Dad sent him to plough one of our old turf pastures that ran alongside the Peover Eye, giving him strict instructions to plough into every corner. Harry's two horses, Prince and Jewel, had got to know him and together they made an experienced team, and Harry found ploughing with them a relaxing job. He followed Dad's instruction and ploughed right up to the side of the big brook, but unfortunately a steep bank gave way and Prince slid down into the brook. Thankfully the reins that joined his head to Jewel snapped, and she managed to stay on her feet and hold the plough from falling on her mate.

Prince landed on his feet but even then he was about six feet below Jewel which put a terrific strain on both the harness and the chains which connected each horse to the main swindle tree and onto the plough. Although both horses remained perfectly quiet, Harry dare not leave them to get help. In his modest way Harry told me how it took a considerable time to release Prince and get him up out of the brook. It gave the neighbours a good chance to nudge each other and have a smile behind Father's back.

By 1937 my parents had been at Cheadle Farm for five years, the really hard time of the brucellosis outbreak was behind them and they were feeling more secure about their future. I could never fully understand where their confidence came from because the Country was still in depression and agricultural prices were still very low. Main crop potatoes were only about £1 per ton which gave a return of about £10 per acre and most other prices were relative to that. The bright side was still the MMB and the fact that there was no limit to milk production. That more than anything gave Dad the urge to look for a larger farm. Although he wanted to produce milk he saw his farming future as a mixed farmer growing a variety of crops, rotating them around the fertility provided by a large dairy herd and, of course, the stability of a monthly milk cheque.

CHAPTER
FIVE

Lower Peover

When I look back I often wonder why my mother was so supportive of my father's wish to move on when she had only been in that house for five years. Although they were hard, demanding years, they were for her very happy ones. Cheadle Farmhouse was built of attractive Cheshire brick and lay amongst leafy winding lanes in lovely countryside. It was not a grand country house but a very comfortable home for a large family of six, plus Grandma Webb and two members of staff.

I have made much about farming being in the blood but Mum wasn't born on a farm. Although many of her relatives were farmers, her father was a shoemaker by trade and in her early years he lived and worked from his home just over the Lower Peover border in Bradshaw Brook. This small hamlet is in the parish of Allostock and within it there is a couple of farms, four or five houses and the Methodist Chapel. Grandfather Webb lived in the third house along from the Chapel and was both a lay preacher and Sunday school teacher there. When Mum was ten years old they moved about four miles to the village of Sproston and took over a small shop there so that he could combine it with his shoemaking.

Grandfather was not kept fully occupied with shoemaking and filled in his time in summer working on nearby farms. In winter he would help his cousin Tia Webb, who spent the winter months trussing hay for a living. Before the age of the bale, hay was usually stacked loose either under cover of an open sided shed or in the open, and often those haystacks were built near to or in the hay field. The hay "trusser" would work freelance for an agreed price per block, moving from farm to farm wherever there was work. He cut the hay into blocks (about the size of a small bale), tied them with string and either he or the farmer would re-stack them in the hay shed or load them onto a hay waggon. It was usually done when the hay had been sold to go off the farm, to another farmer or to a merchant. Remember that then there were the city cows and a massive number of horses in towns and cities, all needing feeding.

When a farmer was feeding his cattle from an outside haystack, he would cut a wedge out from top to bottom leaving the stack still thatched and weather-proof, cutting out further wedges as the winter progressed. The weight of hay in a stack compresses itself until at the bottom it is all most as hard as concrete. When I was young I worked a hay knife a few times and it was back-breaking work, although I am sure that I was short of skill and experience. The hay knife had a flat blade with a curved edge and was about three feet in length. The handle was at a right angle to the blade so that as I plunged the blade straight down into the hay the handle was horizontal. The shape of the knife handle allowed me to put my full weight onto it, but those few hours I spent plunging that three foot blade up and down left me with immense admiration for the men who were fit enough to truss hay for a living.

When Mother was only eighteen she and Grandmother were waiting for Grandad to come in for lunch. He had been digging potatoes with a fork for a neighbouring farmer. The field was only a hundred yards from the little shop so Mum ran upstairs to look out of the bedroom window and to her horror she could see Grandad lying dead by his fork. That left them without a breadwinner, and reliant on their small shop for a living. Mum increased their income by collecting rates. I presume that was how she met Dad because his home was less than two miles down the road, nearer to Holmes Chapel.

Mother had many relatives in the parishes touching onto Lower Peover, some farmers, but others local craftsmen, among them a wheelwright, a tailor and a shoemaker. My Grandma's cousin Sam Harrop kept the post office at Swan Cottage, Hulme Lane, where the present village shop is. The post office was moved to Gough's Timber Yard and later to the Smithy House. He used to walk with the mail to the Finger Post on the A50 in Toft. His brother who was a postman in Knutsford would walk out to Toft to meet up with him to exchange both mail and gossip, and Sam would deliver most of his incoming mail on the way back home. His married daughter, Nellie Bently, lived in a delightful old black and white cottage at Peover Heath called "Portabella Castle", which had at one time been an "ale house", but it was in such a poor condition in 1936 that it was condemned, making the Bentlys' move out. Then the War came and the cottage wasn't demolished, and has since been rebuilt into a lovely black and white cottage.

In later life Nellie Bently became a weekly visitor to my home after she had lost her husband and was living on her own. She and Mother enjoyed each other's company and fortunately I was at an age when I had time to sit and listen. Nellie was a natural story teller and having lived in Lower Peover or Allostock all her life, she was full of delightful tales, many involving our relatives. Alas, I was young and I didn't see the need to write them down, so many have been forgotten. Some I have remembered and woven into this book.

The one I enjoyed the most was about her and Mum's second cousin Miss Harrop. There is another pub still in Lower Peover, the Crown, not in the old village centre, if it has a centre, and in those days it was possible to buy bottles of beer there to take home. Miss Harrop didn't want any one to know about her liking for a bottle of stout, so she regularly went round to the back door of the Crown, bought two bottles and concealed them by tucking them into the top of her stockings under her suspenders, beneath her long skirt, which billowed out and came down almost to the floor — I would have loved to see her hitching her skirt up to tuck one bottle under each suspender. It was the age of the "sit-up-and-beg" bicycle, the handle bars so high

88

that you literally sat upright and pedalled sedately. Nellie Bently was standing by the roadside one day when Miss Harrop came by returning from one of her visits to the Crown. She gave Nellie a dignified greeting and continued on her way, but unfortunately, just as she went past, the pedalling got too much for one of the bottles of stout. The cap blew off and froth exploded out from beneath her skirt. A very embarrassed Miss Harrop had to hurriedly dismount and make an undignified retrieval of the foaming bottle.

The Parish of Lower Peover is interwoven with small leafy lanes, and hidden behind the green hedges were many small country cottages, now mostly rebuilt and extended to more luxurious houses. Unfortunately many of these quite wealthy newcomers wish to remain hidden from the village and do not contribute much to the life of the parish. The result is that not just this, but many villages like it, have lost much of the community spirit and pride of belonging of the past. Residents should have pride in Lower Peover. It is one of the gems of Cheshire; with the Church, the school, the Bells of Peover Hotel and the old Vicarage all along one small cobbled stone lane in a delightful and timeless setting.

Other than the Vicarage the cobbled lane is the most recent of them. It was laid as a coachway in 1730 and is still used today. I suppose it is inevitable in this modern age that someone will twist their ankle on a cobble edge and sue the Council, who in turn will have to tarmac it over or vandalise it in some other way. As it is now, it lies as a memorial to the generations who have trod those stones; from the raucous laughter of school days to the solemn pleasure of the marriage service; from the congenial companionship of an evening at the pub, to the heartbreaking sadness of the funeral cortege.

The school was built in 1710 by the Rev. R. Comberbach. In 1726 he bequeathed £320 for the support of the schoolmaster, with a further sum of £100 for a charity whose profits were to purchase books for the school. This was the school that my brothers and sister attended, but they seldom walked up the cobbles — just occasionally when Dad was driving past, he would drop them off (and later on myself as well) at the end. The rest of the time we would go in the back way down Barrow Brow, crossing the bridge over the Peover Eye into Church Walk, then across the graveyard, through the Lychgate and down the cobbles to the school.

There was a second pub in Church Walk called the Church House. It was almost back to back with the Bells and in fact had been run by the Bell family. Because noisy behaviour was disturbing church services the Church House was closed in 1923. That left the Bells of Peover as the only hotel in that part of the village. Its position is unusual because it lies with its front door facing the graveyard and one side along the old school playground. Today there is a back drive from Church Walk in to the Bells car park but in my youth people had to walk across the graveyard to get into the front door of the pub. More than one vicar, with a dry throat after a lengthy sermon, has made use of that handy door, and as you can imagine there have been one or two interesting experiences when the way home from the pub crosses a graveyard.

There was an occasion when a grave had been dug quite close to the path ready for a burial the next day. It was an accident waiting to happen, and one old chap fell in. As it was a new grave it was well over six feet deep and the old man was neither agile or sober enough to climb out, no matter how he tried. After several fuddled and futile efforts he gave up and curled up in the corner to keep warm. After a while a younger man also fell in, and he too made several attempts but just couldn't get a strong enough grip in the turf on the lip of the grave to heave himself up. When he stopped to look up and think for a moment, a voice from the dark corner of the grave said. "It's no use, lad, I've tried and tried, and I canna get out". The young man immediately took one almighty leap and was gone!

St Oswald's Church is reputed to be one of the most beautiful black and white churches in England. It was built in 1269 by parishioners under the direction of the landlord Richard Grovenour, out of materials at hand — oak, mud and reeds. Through the centuries it has been altered and extended many times. The present stone tower was built in 1562 and the church had a major renovation in 1852. During that major and lengthy renovation, one of the joiners working on the church was Hugh Bolshaw. He obviously enjoyed his pint and working within forty yards of a pub must have seemed like his version of Heaven. He drank a bit too much sometimes and was asked to leave on those occasions. So he bought a grave, with a stone inscribed, conveniently near the back door of the pub, and when asked to leave he would wander out and lie down on his grave declaring that he was on his own ground and no one could move him on. He also bought his own coffin. While he was still alive he used to keep his bread in it.

The Rev. Canon J. C. Sladden wrote a lovely little book "Beside the Bright Stream" which is on sale in the church. In it is much of the colourful history of the church and because this is a story about the people of the area, rather than the buildings, I am not going to write much about a church that really has to be seen to be appreciated. The book tells how the Rev. Arthur Guest, Vicar from 1877 to 1911, first occupant of the now "Old" Vicarage, and in whose time the Lychgate was built, in 1908 had a famous altercation with a party of actors from Manchester who came in 60 motor cars to the Warren de Tably Arms (now the Bells of Peover) and disturbed his Sunday Service. He was also the first person in the parish to buy a car and he was in turn killed in a car accident while on the way to a preaching appointment in September 1911. The six bells were re-hung in his memory in 1912. Willy Lea, sitting chair-bound at the mill, got to know both these bells and the bellringers so well, that he could tell by the sound of them, who was ringing.

Another story from the book tells how in the Rev Arthur Guest's time the sixth centenary was celebrated in 1896 instead of 1869, because of an error in the standard History of Cheshire. On the belfry wall in the church a diamond-shaped tablet reads — "*To the glory of God, in the commemoration of the six-centenary of* this church (1296–1896), and of the Diamond Jubilee of her Majesty Queen Victoria (1837–1897), the clock chimes were placed in the tower on Wake Sunday, 1897". So the mistaken date will hang on the belfry wall to confuse visitors through future generations.

Within its dark oak interior is a massive old trunk or chest, reputed to be even older than the church. It was hewn out of just one oak tree trunk and the lid is formed from the same solid timber. There is an old legend that requires a prospective Cheshire farmer's wife to be able to lift the lid with one hand — I believe that the secret was not to use great strength but for the girl to slide her hand through the large metal handle palm down, then press to take the weight on her forearm and lift from the shoulder. It seems to prove though, that to be a good farmer's wife a girl doesn't need brute force but the knack to make difficult jobs look easy. There is an old saying in Lower Peover that before her marriage a farmer's daughter should be able to make "a loaf without a crease, a cheese without an eye, and twenty pies an hour". It makes you wonder what she had to do for dessert!

The cobbled stone lane was the only way into the Bells of Peover by road. In the old days it was a small village inn called the Warren de Tabley Arms and was owned by the Lords of Tabley. The Bell family had been at the pub a few years before they started to brew their famous beer in 1842, and it is from the family that the present name comes. Although the Church bells often ring over the hotel to add to its charm, it does not derive its name from them.

A Lower Peover scrapbook written just after the War is the source of the story of how the wife of one of the first Bells came from the "Bird in Hand" at Mobberley, bringing with her a recipe for beer. The water used in the beer came from a spring which rose on the other side of the Peover Eye. The spring water flowed down a pipe to a reception tank by the brewery and from there was pumped inside by hand. The beer made to this special recipe, using that lovely spring water, was supplied to several other pubs in Cheshire (I have heard numbers from eight to twenty eight). Whatever the truth, it must have been of rare quality to attract such widespread acclaim.

The brewery became so famous that in 1871, George Bell, who had been making beer for nearly thirty years, was asked to go to Hillsborough Castle in Ireland on the occasion of the birth of the Sixth Marquis of Downshire. He was asked to make a special brew to be tapped twenty-one years later in 1892. The ale was placed in hogheads and bricked up in a cellar below the castle so that it was hermetically sealed. Knowing how the Irish love beer, it was a wise move. Ten years later, George Bell jun. went over to Ireland to open it up to see that the ale was standing the test of time.

Then in 1892, the same George Bell was sent for to tap the beer to celebrate the twenty-first birthday of the young Marquis. Four thousand friends and tenants drank his health in the ale. The "Lisburn Herald" on July 9th 1892 reported the event as follows. "Several connoisseurs compared it to rich sparkling cider, and gave it as their opinion that the ingredients employed in its manufacture must have been of the purest description, and the scientific manipulation of the same was all that could be desired."

The beer brought people from afar to the Bells. In the scrapbook Mrs Evelyn Nowel related how as a small girl before the motor car, she watched landaus, bearing gentlemen in shining top hats and ladies in beautiful dresses, arrive at the Bells Hotel for tea every weekend in summer. Some people would arrive in Knutsford by train, then hire horse-drawn carriages from Hardy's livery stables behind the Royal George Hotel to make the three mile journey to Lower Peover.

The Bells became a large and influential family in the area. Running what was in those days a large brewery business and also farming Mill Bank Farm, kept many of the family members involved. Around 1900 there were six members of the Bell family, and seven members of the Gough family, in the Lower Peover church choir, with a Gough as the choirmaster. It was claimed to be a record throughout the British Isles.

The Bell family success was to be touched with sadness when one very attractive daughter was not allowed to marry the man of her choice. The family decided he wasn't good enough. Finally they persuaded her to marry someone else, but she became so unhappy she committed suicide. In fact I believe there are two unmarked (suicide) graves in the churchyard that relate to that sad period in the Bell family's time at Lower Peover.

The other businesses in the village were situated around or near to the village green or, as it is now called, the Smithy Green. It is a triangular patch of grass with the Smithy lying on one side, between the B5081 and what was the old salter's road which for centuries carried the packhorses loaded with salt from Northwich to Macclesfield, and even further across the Pennines towards Sheffield and the East.

Arnold Jackson followed his father to the Smithy, and he was the smith from the mid-1930s and through the War. With his smithy opening onto the green it meant there was often an audience watching him work — or more, to his annoyance, distracting him from his work. Across the Salter's Lane from the Smithy was the former home of the thrashing machine proprietor Samual Carter Lea, by then occupied by his grandson, Harry Gough. About a hundred yards up the road was the timber merchants James Gough and Sons. The three sons were Henry and Peter, who worked in the timber yard, making almost anything that could be made from wood, and Harry, who ran the business, bought and sold the timber, and felled the trees that supplied both their yard and others.

Both the families were related to the Leas at the mill and were part of my father's farming life. Harry Gough in particular had an influence on Dad's future, so I will tell you a little about their history. Theophilis Lea (I kid you not) left the family business at Lower Peover mill about the middle of the nineteenth century to build up his own provender business in Manchester and he branched out into the import and export of both provender and tea. Back in the nineteenth century, tea was an expensive product and it took big money to deal in it. To be nearer the action he moved his operation to the Port of Liverpool, and his business grew until he became a wealthy merchant. That wealth was built on big money deals at high risk, but somewhere along the line one went wrong — although I suspect it was more likely that Theophilis himself went wrong. To be kind to him, we don't know what started his troubles; perhaps a ship sank or some such mishap took place. Whatever the cause he both turned to drink and became bankrupt.

By the time the Peover members of the family heard about the collapse of the merchant business and the subsequent loss of their home, the three sons of Theophilis were in a workhouse in Liverpool. I suspect their father may have been in jail, although the family history is understandably vague. Certainly Theophilis ended up in the workhouse himself and in there contacted typhus and died in the workhouse hospital.

Theophilis' wife was the daughter of a Lach Dennis farmer, Samuel Carter, although the family believed that she had died before the business collapse. When Samuel Carter heard of the boys' troubles, he decided that he must help. He walked the four miles to Old Hartford station, then travelled by train to Liverpool, where he walked to try to find the workhouse where they were staying. He eventually found the two younger boys John Henry and William barefoot and almost in rags. The oldest boy, Samuel Carter Lea (born 1855 and named after his Grandad) was in his early teens and a few minutes later came running down the street with a fish hidden under his shirt, which he had just stolen it from the market — their only food.

Samuel Carter took them shopping for clothes and shoes, then to the bathhouse where they washed and changed into their new clothes before going on to a restaurant to enjoy the meal of a lifetime. When they arrived back at Hartford station the first thing that the boys did was to take off their new boots and walk barefoot back to the Farm at Lach Dennis.

The youngest boy, William, dropped out of the family history, (perhaps he died soon after going to the farm) but the other two were sent to school at Northwich at the expense of their Grandfather. The boys were made to work on the farm before and after school. The family claim that Grandad Carter set his grandfather clock forward two hours so that he could get more work out of them before they walked to school. That clock is still in the family and I believe it is still kept the same two hours fast in memory. When they had finished their schooling they worked for him on the farm until they were both in their twenties when they got the idea to start a contracting business thrashing corn for other farmers and old Samual Carter, bless him, financed their first machinery purchase in 1876.

Before the thrashing machine, separating grain had been done by the back-breaking hand flailing and winnowing technique used almost unchanged from biblical times. Although the thrashing box ended the "near mind destroying" drudgery of the old method, it was resented by the poorer, less skilled farm workers because of the loss of their work. The thrashing box was no small machine and it was driven by a steam engine that couldn't propel itself. The engine was mounted on a strong four-wheel waggon, pulled from farm to farm, like any other horse drawn carriage. In fact moving all the thrashing machinery was a major operation; neighbouring farmers would join in with their teams of horses to pull the steam engine, the thrashing box and the battener.

When working, one man stood on top of the thrashing box to cut open the un-thrashed sheaves and feed them into mouth of the thrashing box. If he was careful to feed them in crossways, and with the butt end of each sheaf to the same side of the box, then the thrashed straw would come through the thrasher more or less unbroken. That was important because only straight straw could be used or sold for thatching. The battener re-tied the thrashed straw into very large sheaves, which were in fact called battens. Standing at the end of the thrashing box, the battener caught the straw as it came out if the man on top had done his job well, with hardly a straw broken.

There were few open-sided (dutch) barns in those days so the corn was usually built into a group of stacks in what became known as the stackyard. Those stacks would be thatched with some of the straw from the year before and some of the present year's carefully thrashed straw would be stacked and kept dry for thatching each new stack at the next harvest. Although some farmers did their own thatching, there were many professional men skilled in the craft who made their living this way. In the summer there would be haystacks to thatch, in the autumn corn stacks and through the rest of the year there were farm buildings and cottages to repair or re-roof.

The thrashing tackle would stay at each farm for a few days depending on the number of stacks to be thrashed; a decision based on the grain market or the farmer's need of straw or grain, or even money. The four or five extra men with the machinery would have to be fed and looked after by the farmer's wife, feeding them at midday on boiled potatoes and turnip, with meat if they had it, or made into potato hash (hotpot), when the men would search for their bit of meat amongst the potatoes and turnip. This was followed by apple dumpling made in a muslin cloth. Later in the day "door-step sized" cheese butties were handed round at "baggin" time (tea break), or perhaps after the thrashing stopped for the day. They would then have them for tea, with a jam buttie for sweet. It was a time of excitement on each farm, with the young boys carrying water, logs and coal to the engine, and the girls taking drinks around for the men and everyone joining in the rat-catching sport towards the bottom of each stack.

The two Lea brothers' business soon grew and another thrashing machine was bought, followed by a third. Each set of thrashing tackle needed a team of three or four men — in addition farmers would often lend each other an extra man or two. The turnover made Samuel Carter Lea and John Henry Lea into successful business men. With all those machines to maintain there was a constant need of a blacksmith so the Lea family moved their base near to Smithy Green and the blacksmith and his forge. Bearings were simple brass bushes which gradually wore away and needed to be replaced quite often. The major repair time was in the summer prior to the next harvest when the machines were not in use, when every possible breakdown had to be anticipated and prevented by replacing worn or weak parts. Once the thrashing season got under way breakdowns cost double — the cost of the repair plus the bigger cost of lost working time. New bearings were very tight when fitted and needed to be "run in" so it was not unusual in summer for there to be two or three steam engines by the Green, running all day. When they were just "running in" bearings on the steam engine, they would tick over very quietly but when they were driving the thrashing tackle there was great noise.

Their first self-propelled steam engine was a Marshall bought in 1908, and soon after they bought the first traction engine that Fodens made. The two families became good friends by the time they purchased a second Foden's traction engine. At the peak of their business at Smithy Green they sold bicycles, sowing machines, black cast iron oven ranges and fireplaces, ploughs and harrows. In fact with the post office and shop there also it was a hive of activity supplying both house and farm.

The people who live in Lower Peover today seem keen to retain it as a quiet sleepy village as they imagine it has always been. If they could have visited it at the turn of the twentieth century, the noise and the activity would have frightened them. The blacksmith's hammer banged away above the "chuck chuck" of two or three steam engines, whilst the scream of the bandsaw from James Gough's timberyard just 100 yards up the road would have drowned most conversations. The number of people doing business around the green, or going down Free Green Lane to the Mill, would have been considerable.

By the 1930s the thrashing machines were not so dependent on the Smithy and the business had been moved to Boots Green, on the border of Lower Peover and Over Peover, where it was run for some years by Samuel's son George Henry. Tragically he died in mid-life in 1935 when his son George was only fifteen years old. Young George and his mother kept the thrashing business, with the three steam engines, going for many years.

Samual Carter Lea's daughter Margeret married James Gough. Although in the past the Gough family appear to have been blacksmiths and wheelwrights, now they were just in timber. Their son Harry also had two sons, Jim and Geoff, who helped in their father's business and were very much part of the village life. The old farm building that still stands just across the road from the Smithy had a thatch roof — well, it did have until the Gough boys were sharing a secret woodbine one evening after tea — now it has a slate roof. They both still swear that they were careful not to cause a spark but any thatched roof is a fire hazard, and that one went up with a woosh just after they had walked away from it!

The two boys would run down to the timberyard most evenings after school and if one of their uncles, Henry or Peter, needed to work on the hand-driven lathe, he would persuade one of them to turn it. The turning wheel was too heavy for a boy to start it off but if Henry or Peter got the speed up, a boy could keep it going and as a reward they would turn a yo-yo for him.

Certainly the business life of that village, so close to our farm, made an important contribution to my father's farming operation. In his search for a larger farm he always took the availability of access and services into account. In 1938 he and Mother at last saw the farm they really wanted, the Finger Post Farm in the next parish of Toft. Standing on the A50 road but still less than two miles from the centre of Lower Peover, it seemed to be everything they dreamt of. Toft estate was owned by the Leycester family and their agent Mr Hall wanted a reference so he asked Harry Gough to give his assessment of my father. Before the motor car created so much mobility, the lives of the occupants of a country village were so entwined that they knew each others' business and in Lower Peover the main families were also related to the extent that there would be no secrets untold. I am sure that Harry Gough would know just what my Dad was worth, if he owed any money and even how he stood at the bank. He would certainly know how good a farmer he was reputed to be. Although Harry Gough was seriously ill with cancer, he managed to give the reference needed to enable my parents to take over the tenancy of Finger Post Farm in the Spring of 1939.

There was a lot of excitement at Cheadle Farm when my parents got that news. I hadn't seen Finger Post Farm so I had not realised that there was a house there and I spent a considerable time trying to work out how our house could be moved. I suppose I got the idea from the hens. It was simple really; Dad moved our hens on to the stubble fields as soon as the sheaves of wheat or oats had been carted into the stackyard. I had watched the men taking down the sectional hen cotes, then rebuilding them out on the stubble fields so the hens could eat any spilled grain — the action of the binder and all the hand work to stook, load and cart each field of corn shed a lot of grain. It sounds good economics but the reality was very different. The hens had to be released each morning and shut up again at night and the hens would not go inside their cotes until dusk. If you went too early they would still be outside and if you went just a few minutes too late, the fox would be out on his rounds and an open hen cote was the highlight of his life.

So I just presumed that we moved like the hens, and would take our house with us. To take my mind off the problem, Dad suggested that I went for a ride in the car with him. He had decided to hire Tom Riley with his milk lorry to haul some of our farm equipment from one farm to the other. When we got to Tom's house at Hulme Mill, Dad left me in the car whilst he went to the house, but he soon came dashing back saying, "Tom has just gone round to see me; if we hurry back we should catch him." But Tom Riley had got the same message from Mum and, yes, it had to happen! The lane was narrow with overgrown thorn hedges on either side and on one of the sharp bends the two old cars came head to head, their lovely silvery radiators mashed together and steam billowing up through the morning air. I wasn't hurt and was told to stay in the car but through the steam I could see a lot of arm waving generating even more steam. I presume Father's temper got the better of him even with a close neighbour and friend.

CHAPTER
SIX

Our Move to Toft

Father's new farm was again double the size, which meant a move up from 80 to over 160 acres and at last I was taken to see it. The house was very large and tall, with a black and white gable end to one side of the front elevation, and a lovely wooden porch over the front door in the middle.

The front part of the house contained two large lounges downstairs, with a long straight staircase leading to two equally large bedrooms above and two large and one small bedroom in the older back part. Those front rooms had been built in the second half of the nineteenth century, whilst the rear of the farm house was probably seventeenth century. With lower ceilings in the old half there was four steps between the two parts upstairs. A back set of stairs led up to two more large bedrooms, in fact one of them was over the old bakehouse and would hold six single beds with ease.

The farm was a small boy's dream home. Not only was the house large and rambling, the garden was also large and overgrown, and there was a deep sided brook at the bottom, which caused my mother some worry.

The range of old style brick farm buildings seemed enormous, especially as most of them had a tall hay loft above. The main drawback to our new farm was the busy A50 road past the gate which was dangerous even in those days. Coming from a quiet leafy green lane, that road was a noisy nightmare for both us and our farm animals; as time went by we found out that it was only the cats who lived through their first accident who then had the road sense to stay alive. About seventy acres of our land lay across the road, which meant that livestock farming for us was always fraught with anxiety; especially as forty acres of that was the only permanent pasture on the farm that was not ploughed up.

One interesting feature was just how flat the farm was. Toft brook ran along the bottom of the garden, some sixteen feet below both garden and field level. At the top end of the farm, about three-quarters of a mile further up stream, it was no more than five feet below ground level. Just before the brook flowed past the garden it ran through some old pit-holes, now dry, and those allowed the cows a low bank to drink from. But other than that the brook was really a deep sided hand dug dyke and most of the land on either side of it was dead flat, the brook flowing on in absolutely straight line through what at some time must have been a large marsh.

The soil on that flat area was hardly peat but it was what we in Cheshire call mossy (in fact the next farm was called Moss Farm), that quick drying, black soil which held its moisture in dry seasons, yet was so easily

107

worked that it could be safely described as a "boy's soil" — it didn't need a lot of skill to manage it. The down side of this very good farm was that almost every field touched a wood somewhere, some with woods on more than one side. Not only were crop yields reduced around their margins, but those large blocks of woodland sheltered us from winds and made crops slow to dry at harvest time.

To farm those extra acres Dad had to buy in more stock machinery, and with some urgency, one extra horse to work the land. Buying a genuine, sound and experienced working horse was very difficult. If they were good then their owners were not likely to part with them; on the other hand, if a horse had a fault then the owner would not be likely to tell anyone about it. Dad didn't want to bother with an inexperienced colt so when he heard about a very good horse whose owner was short of money, he quickly went to look and in fact bought a good looking and tall horse called Captain. Bred from the Clydesdale breed, Captain stood taller than our other two horses; his long legs could stride out at a pace that made him an ideal horse for road work.

At Finger Post the retiring tenant Franky Beswick had kept a good path through the woods to the Dun Cow at Ollerton, but other than that the farm had become very derelict. For a few years Mr Robinson (it was not uncommon to address a worker with formality) had been the only man working on the farm and with just one pair of horses, there was a lot he could not do. There were many rabbits on the farm, both in the woods and along the hedge rows. Mr Robinson's two horses didn't like to walk over rabbit holes — I think it was the way a rabbit hole could collapse under the horse's foot which made them afraid; so when ploughing he would turn back when his horses came to a rabbit hole near to the fence. As the years went by the rabbits dug further out in the fields and the horses turned back further from the fence, and some fields had ten to fifteen yards of unploughed land around the outsides on which briars and hawthorn had started to grow. You can imagine what Dad thought and said about such a waste of good land, so Harry had to clear it before he could plough.

The new tenancy began on March 20th, but as there had been no ploughing done on Finger Post Farm that winter the agent agreed for Dad to have early entry. Since the old tenancy on Cheadle Farm didn't run out until the same day, it meant that he had to plough all the arable land on that farm as well. When a tenant leaves a farm, all his improvements including increased soil fertility are valued in his favour, but offset against that money is the potential cost of correcting all the faults such as blocked ditches or drains, broken gates or fences etc; and any unploughed arable land would be included in this. The end result means that a good farmer should draw an outgoing payment, whereas a bad farmer had to pay dilapidation fees to his old landlord. Dad wanted his outgoing money so he ploughed at Cheadle Farm with Prince and Jewel, whilst Harry Davies took Captain each day with a small load of equipment to our new farm at Toft.

Captain was supposed to be almost fault-free but Harry soon found that his new horse did not like a motor lorry overtaking him. When one came up behind him he would be off unless Harry had a firm hold. Harry got used to this quirk in the horse and anticipated any danger well in advance. There was one return trip on an afternoon when Captain had relaxed and munched hay throughout the day while Harry had worked hard in the fields, so the horse was fresh but Harry was tired. Captain seemed in a good mood as Harry harnessed him back into the shafts and then jumped onto the front of the light four-wheeled lorry, expecting to sit and relax on the journey home. Captain strode out for home, and there was only about fifty yards to travel along the A50 main road before he turned down the slope into the Lower Peover road. As Captain turned down the bank, the lorry pushed against him and its iron tyres rattled on the road, Captain must have thought that something was coming up behind him, so he "went". The lorry bumped and rattled, the iron wheels clattered, but Harry held the reins like a stage coach driver as Captain went at full gallop for home.

One of our new neighbours was Tom Lea whose farm was the next one down the lane, and he and his man Harry Royle were working in a roadside field where they stood watching in amazement as Captain, with his long legs stretching out, flashed past. They would have a story to tell in the pub that night. Fortunately Harry could still control his direction but he didn't manage to slow him down. It was not until

110

they came to Lower Peover Smithy over one and a half miles down the road, that Captain dropped down to his long striding walk, just as though nothing had happened.

The estate that our farm was on has been in the Leycester family for over nine hundred years, passing down on three occasions through the female line. It is one of the oldest direct blood lines among the landowning families in Cheshire and the present family are rightly proud of their heritage. Ralph Leycester inherited the estate in 1809 but sadly died when only thirty four years old, leaving five children. In his short life he had managed to make a fortune in India and he spent some of it making considerable alterations to Toft Hall. He must also have planned and financed a new church at Toft because it was finished in 1855, only four years after his death. Before then the Leycesters had worshipped at Lower Peover.

Ralph's son, Ralph Oswald, inherited at the age of seven in 1851 and lived to the ripe old age of 85. He married, but he died in 1929 without issue. His brother was drowned at sea, also without issue, so the estate passed down the female line to Osmund Ralph Maude Roxby, Sub-Dean, Cannon and Rector of Truro Cathedral. (In 1949 he devised succession to his only son Edmund, who in 1957 assumed for himself and issued by Royal Licence the surname and arms of Leycester.)

The reality was that there was no resident landlord at Toft for a very long time, although the Hall had in the past been the family home, Ralph Oswald had lived in

London and only visited Toft for spells through the year. He maintained a full staff and kept the estate in good order; there were four or five gardeners, six domestic staff, two coachmen, two gamekeepers and four or five men working in the woods and maintaining the farm properties. One wing of the Hall had twelve bedrooms which were used just to house the people who worked either in the Hall or on the estate.

When Ralph was staying at the Hall his wife believed in keeping up appearances. When she wanted to go into Knutsford she insisted the coachmen took her in the four in hand coach — she said that anything less than four horses would give the wrong impression. She never travelled the most direct route but went across the main road, past Toft church and out to Ollerton on a gravel lane through the Windmill Wood (now known as Toft Woods). There was another coach lane going the back way from the Hall, past the walled garden and across Ullard Hall Farm to Lower Peover; and although the estate was only about 2500 acres, those private lanes meant that the owners could take long coach rides through their own attractive fields and woods.

Harry Beswick (who later married Mother's cousin) was the son of the estate tenant on Heeson Green Farm. On leaving school just before the First World War, he worked as an apprentice gardener at Toft Hall. In my own youth he told me some details of how the house and gardens had been run. There was a superb walled garden, growing a wide range of vegetables and fruit, with heated greenhouses producing exotic fruits. The drive to the Hall crossed the lake over a stone

112

bridge, and in his youth he helped to net fish from the lake for the Squire's table, setting the net under the arch of the bridge. A large brick ice house was built under one bank of the lake and in winter Harry helped to cut ice and fill the deep well inside. When there was sufficient ice on the water they started cutting it from the middle of the lake, and would work backwards towards the ice house. Lying on ladders for safety and using long iron hooks to pull the blocks of ice up onto the ice sheet, they would slide them across the surface back to the ice house on the bank. The ice house is still there, hidden deep under the ground, with trees growing above for shade.

The ice would remain frozen throughout the summer and whole carcasses of beef were amongst the food stored down there. It must have been a super deep freeze but there was a disadvantage — it was about two hundred yards away from the Hall, so if the Squire insisted on a cold drink in the middle of the night, the butler had a problem. His nightshirt would be flapping round his ankles as he made the dash.

Of course the Sub-Dean lived in Truro but after inheriting the estate he visited not just the estate, but each individual tenant every year. My sister Mary remembers one visit just after we had moved to the farm. The landlord had sent a request to have afternoon tea with us and Mary had to take a day off school to wait on the Sub-Dean and his party. The front lounge was seldom used but it was that day, along with the best china. Mary served homemade butter and homemade jam; there were wafer thin sandwiches and delicate cakes that had Dad grunting with derision. The Dean and his wife were delightful people and gained the respect of all their tenants, as their son Edmund has also done in later years — but that is for a later story.

The estate was heavily wooded, not just narrow shelter belts, but large blocks of mature trees giving a patchwork quilt of colours as the varied species sprang to life in spring, and again in the late summer as they changed to their autumn hue. By 1939 all that was left of the estate maintenance staff was two elderly brothers, Bill and Tom Gresty, working mostly in the woods, as had their father before them. Their work was more than just maintaining the woods; they also kept the main waterways clean and repaired the landlord's fences.

Across the road, our one block of permanent pasture was mostly peat; in fact some of our Irish workers would dry a few pieces to burn on their fire in nostalgic memory of home. A series of springs welled both in our field and through the woods on each side, creating small streams that had to be kept clean or both our field and the woodland would soon become waterlogged. The peat soil became a quagmire where water lay on it, so it was impossible to stand in those ditches and brooks, even with wellington boots on. As these old men only wore strong leather boots, they had to devise a way of working without sinking in the bog. They built a sledge each, just like a child's snow sledge, about two foot long by a foot wide, on which they stood to dig. They had a length of rope to the front of it; when one of them wished to move his sledge along he would

114

place one foot against each bank and straddle the ditch, then pull the sledge along about two feet. He would step back on to the sledge and dig out the two feet behind it, and then repeat the whole process to move up again. Those two old men had been digging out those brooks and ditches each winter throughout their lives and as a result had become more than a little taciturn. They treated small inquisitive boys with disdain, so I regret that although they must have had interesting stories to tell, none came my way.

The really heavy timber work done on the estate was done by James Gough and Sons. Through the years they had relied on timber from both the Toft and Tabley estates to supply most of their needs at the timber yard. Their needs were varied; under the direction of Henry and Peter Gough who supervised that side of the business, they made an incredible range of products from coffins to horse carts. To increase their range they had to import some timber which came in to Plumley Station on open trucks. They never knew when a shipment might arrive, but once they were notified it had arrived at the station they would be given a day to remove it, after which they were charged a rent for each day it remained unmoved. By 1939 Harry Gough's son Jim was nearly thirty and had been running the tree felling side of the business for many years (he claims that he bought his first oak tree when he was only nine years old). When he got the message that a shipment was in, he would have to stop whatever work he was doing and take all his men, horses and timber waggons to haul the imported wood back to the yard.

115

That timber had travelled uncovered in all weathers so it needed many months of drying before use, and for this it was stacked in a large open barn in the yard, spaced so that it could dry out naturally but stacked so that it couldn't warp. Jim derides the kiln-dried timber used today, because in his experience it may be dry but it can still warp; he believes that timber needs to dry slowly over many months and only then will it stay true.

The woods at Toft had been planted at different times so the Goughs were able to select mature trees on an ongoing basis. The hardness and durability of the British oak made it the most important of all the timber they used. Jim showed me a photo of what I thought was a massive oak, but he claimed that many were that size in those days. When I asked him why then had nearly all the maturing oak on my farm gone "stag-headed" (dead bows in their crown which destroys their timber value) before they reached 150 years of age, he explained his belief that it was caused by atmospheric pollution in the late nineteenth and early twentieth centuries. Now with much less pollution we may again see oaks growing healthily for 200 years, when they become really large.

On the way to Manchester Jim would have to haul timber through the main street in Knutsford. He claims to be the only man to have done this with horses (often a string of five), steam engine, motor lorry, and also with a hand cart, which he did for fun one Knutsford Mayday. Five horses pulling a sixty-foot length of timber would take a bit of handling through the narrow streets of Knutsford, but a steam engine would seem really modern and progressive. Although a steam engine had its limits in the timber business — it couldn't go across soft land — with a winch on it became an important tool for them.

Before the War Toft Hall had been let to a Dr Doherty who ran a health farm; yes, carrot juice and massage are not so new after all! The difference this made was in and around the Hall; although the walled gardens were no longer used, and the ice house was redundant, the flower gardens were maintained and the Hall was lived in. The woodlands were managed as before, with Jim Gough selecting mature trees and agreeing a price with the estate agent before felling them. On one occasion Gough's had felled some very large oak trees alongside the drive in the park. They were using the winch on the steam engine to load the trees, and as each trunk weighed from six to eight tons they could only roll them on. That was done by rapping a chain several times around each end of the trunk, and placing the timber waggon along side the tree. They then laid two strong skids from the waggon down to the side of the tree trunk. It was a simple matter now to connect the wire rope from the steam engine to the two chains and pull. As the winch wound the rope in, it unwound the chains from the trunk and of course rolled it up the skids.

With eight tons of tree rolling up two planks there was a lot that could go wrong, and this kept everyone's attention on the tree. Suddenly they realised that a van was coming down the drive and the tree was on one side of the drive and the steam engine on the other,

117

which meant that the wire rope was across it. Both Gough brothers rushed out waving their arms but the local butcher's son, George Taylor, was so fascinated with the steam engine that he didn't see either the wire rope or the hand-waving. He hit the rope without touching his brakes and the impact loaded the tree with a thud but the elasticity in the rope catapulted young George's van back about thirty yards up the drive. Fortunately the rope had caught the radiator; had it gone over the radiator it would have cut the cab off and the lad's head with it.

Foxhunting was an important sport for the gentry and Toft's many woods were home to a lot of foxes. The estate placed hunting before its tenants to the extent that the Goughs were brought in each autumn to dismantle all wire fences bordering the woods before the start of the foxhunting season. The fences were not be put up again until hunting had finished in the spring. The estate paid for Goughs to do the work, but the task was so large that they had to take on extra labour to get the many miles of fences dismantled and then replaced or renewed. The problem for the tenant farmer was that he couldn't use any of those fields for his stock throughout the winter months. Our farm being surrounded by woods would have been the worst affected, but the war came just after we moved there and put an end to that practice.

When I was researching this book I visited Jim just a couple of months before he sadly died. He had just been watching Swampy and company protesting over the proposed Second Manchester Airport Runway, and

Jim got very excited about it. He went on to tell me how he had cleared the timber before the first runway was built, with not one protester on the site. Goughs had been awarded the contract through the Toft Estate land agent Herbert Hall who was also the agent for the airport land. (He lived on the estate by Ringway in the old black and white farm house which now has come down to make way for the second runway.) There were a lot of mature trees for Gough's to clear, some sold to merchants in Manchester and the rest hauled back to their yard at Lower Peover. This hauling was done with their team of five horses.

Old Ned Jones was teamsman for Goughs. He was quite a character, living in a small wooden shed inside the timber yard to be next to his horses. Jim Gough still claims that he was one of the best teamsmen in the County. When the horses had to stay at the airport overnight, Ned slept under the manger in front of Prince, his favourite horse. Prince had a colourful past in that he had been condemned to be slaughtered for killing a man in Oldham; Harry Gough got to hear, in a chance conversation with a vet, about this beautiful horse that had to be killed. He went by train from Knutsford, inspected the horse, and listened to the story of how the horse had run away and trapped a man against a lamp post, killing him. Harry Gough decided the horse could be "straightened out", so he bought him for less than quarter of the normal price. Ned took him out on the road for the first time to deliver a load of sawn timber on a small four wheel lorry; as they went along Plumley Moore a slight noise frightened Prince and he bolted. Prince did not bolt straight down the road like Captain had but blindly to the left, where lorry, timber and horse landed in the ditch. But now Ned knew his fault.

It would be nice to tell you how he whispered something in the horse's ear and cured him, but the reality was that Ned took a pick-axe handle and got into position by the horse for Jim to give the horse a fright. I do not know whether he sat on the left shaft or if he stood in front of Prince, but whichever, he had just a split second to land one good blow on the side of Prince's head. If he missed he could easily have been killed or badly hurt himself, and Prince would go off to Donkey Warberton's knacker yard for dog meat. One blow was enough, Prince did not run blindly to the left again, and became the favourite horse of both Ned and his boss Harry Gough. I suppose if Ned did the same thing today he would have be locked up, because it would be hard to explain that that one blow actually saved that horse from the knacker's yard. Ned and that horse became such good friends, not only did Ned sleep under his manger, he also shared his chewing tobacco with him. If Ned was chewing a plug, Prince would keep nuzzling him until he gave him the left-overs.

Jim Gough and old Ned would spend two or three days working with the other staff felling trees on the airport site, then load some to bring them back to the yard, stay at home over night and return to the airport the following morning. On one occasion when they had loaded some large oak trees ready for the return

120

journey they discovered that a part of the brake system on the waggon was missing, but Jim decided they could still make the journey home with an improvised brake. He rigged up a chain from the axle of the waggon to reach across the iron tyre on one of the wooden rear wheels, with the other end fastened to one of the oak trees on the waggon. Ned could walk behind with a crowbar in the chain and tighten it onto the wheel like a tourniquet. Although there were five horses in the team to pull the load up hill, there was only one in the shafts to hold the waggon back down hill. The other four were hitched in front of each other with chains and could only pull forwards. That one horse could normally hold the empty waggon without brakes and even loaded it could control it on slight inclines, so Ned's crowbar would only be needed on a few occasions on the way home.

The only steep bank was at the start of the journey on the A538, which now comes under the runway and that was much steeper than it is now. Nevertheless, Jim was quite confident that they could handle it so he led the horses whilst Ned worked the crowbar. It got a bit interesting. The shaft horse was being pushed down too quickly, bumping into the chain horses in front, and causing them to bunch. Jim had great difficulty in keeping them in line without getting them tangled in their chains, so he had no time to see how Ned was doing at the back until they reached the bottom and stopped the team. He found that the friction between the iron tyre and the chain had been so great that the heat had set the wheel on fire. Fortunately they always had some buckets hanging under the waggon to water their horses with, so there was a panic to find water to put the fire out. There was a brook, but it was the other side of a thick thorn hedge and Jim had to charge his way through to get his water. They managed to put the fire out before the wheel was too badly damaged and they were then able to make an incident-free journey back through Wilmslow and Toft to Lower Peover.

That was a story from the past. Jim Gough was back working in the woods at Toft when we moved there in the early spring of 1939 and I thought the move was "great". There was so much action and excitement; and, yes, I had finally realised that we were not moving the house, but everything else had to be moved. Tom Ryley helped with his milk lorry, Harry with the team of horses; there was a cattle-waggon moving stock; all far more interesting than what was happening to the furniture.

There was still many things that Dad wanted for his larger farm. One was a wider furrowed turn-over plough to make it worth ploughing with three horses and there was one at a nearby farm dispersal sale, so Mother took me along for a day out. In the junk pile was a glass fronted wooden case which had a red squirrel, a peewit, a chaffinch and a starling, all stuffed and mounted in the most realistic way — and I was hooked. Dad was trying to pretend that he was not really interested in the plough, he knew that if he showed too much interest the seller could get a friend to bid against Dad, so he showed no more than a casual interest. But that wasn't easy with a small boy asking him to look at something else. He resolved it by telling me that I couldn't have it, so shut up! In the end a family friend earned Dad's wrath by buying the birds for me. On the way home Mum and Dad had an argument over the fact that this friend had given me the case when Dad had said that I could not have it. I sat on the back seat, my stuffed birds by my side and kept quiet.

I treasured that case, particularly the red squirrel. It was to stand in my bedroom throughout my school days, and although it was put away in the attic for a few years, it came out again to sit in my oldest son's bedroom through most of his school years and now sits on a shelf in my workshop. Would you believe that earlier this year, after nearly sixty years of safe keeping, I put my hand on the glass front whilst I reached a small piece of wood from the shelf above, and broke the glass.

Dad got his wide furrowed David Sleete turn-over plough. It could plough a fourteen inch furrow which was about three inches wider than he could plough before, but it needed a team of three horses to pull it. In the past Franky Beswick had only ploughed about four to five inches deep. Dad was convinced that soil should be ploughed a least eight inches, so Harry Davies set the plough to disturb soil that "had never seen the light of day before".

Captain proved to have another fault in that he too refused to cross the rabbit holes that had intruded into each field margin. Harry solved the problem by hitching Captain in the middle between Prince and

Jewel; they were rock steady in almost any situation and strode on across the holes without hesitation. Captain fastened in between them had little option but to go along. He was never happy though and even after ploughing for a few weeks, if Harry hitched him on the outside he would stop at a rabbit hole.

Two horses could plough an acre each day, but even with the wide plough and three in the team Harry could only plough an extra quarter of an acre. After that they were too tired to do more so Harry couldn't extend the day with a bit of overtime. With about sixty acres to plough in the first year Dad had to bring in extra help. When Harry had ploughed the fields on which corn was to be grown, he started to work and sow them. Dad hired a contractor with a Ford tractor to plough the field on which he was to grow potatoes. It was old grass turf that Father said "had not been ploughed since Adam was a lad". Harry can still remember the mass of stringy roots that would have tired his team of horses but the tractor was tireless. There was a problem though, and that was the fact that it was the first tractor seen working in that area and there still wasn't a purpose-made tractor plough, so the turn-over horse plough was used. Can you imagine the time it would take to turn round at the end of each furrow. Between the two men they had to unhook the tractor; the ploughman then turned the plough over whilst the driver did a very wide three point turn and reversed up to hook the plough on again. After all that, one man had to walk behind the plough holding the handles to steady it, just as he would if following a team

124

of horse. The benefit was that it was relentless, not limited like the horses to a short working day, but I would hate to have been the chap following that plough from dawn to dusk each day.

CHAPTER
SEVEN

The War Began

The War began in September with its terrible effects on so many lives. Now I am not going to write about it in any chronological order, but I would like to just tell you some of the experiences of the people around me, in particular those you have already met in earlier chapters.

On our farm, summer of 1939 saw potato prices still depressed. The early crop that Dad grew on the old turf didn't return as much as he had expected; perhaps they were planted too late to catch the early season high prices. Father made his early potato fields produce two crops, and they had been under planted with ox cabbage for cattle feed. This was how he grew his two crops. Once the early potatoes were in leaf he went through them with the drill plough to "draw them up", which puts more soil onto each potato drill, this hopefully smothered any weeds without covering over the young potato leaves. He then planted ox cabbage plants down alternate drills, these would have to grow in among the potato tops and grew quite leggy as they competed for the light. Then when the potatoes were got in, in June or early July, some soil was pushed around each plant stem, leaving the young cabbage sitting firmly on the ground. By then they were growing very quickly so they grew into very big cabbage by winter. Big, in ox cabbage terms, is really large, many of them would weigh 20lbs and some years later I weighed one of 40lbs. The one drawback was that no mechanical digger could be used in among the cabbage, so those potatoes had to be dug by hand. Early potatoes have such a delicate skin that it was best to dig them carefully with a fork anyway and the skilled labour was available for that type of work.

Through the war years Dad kept a record of all his crops, livestock numbers, and sales at Finger Post, but he didn't keep a record of his sales in the summer of 1939. He often marvelled though, that the ox cabbage he had grown for cattle feed were more valuable than the potatoes that he had sold off the same ground. The War changed everything. Those large, heavy ox cabbages had a coarse strong leaf that would not look very attractive on a modern supermarket shelf, but they were ready for use just after the War started and were all sold for human consumption.

The other half of Dad's potato field was planted with late varieties, which were not dug until Autumn when some were sold straight off the field; the rest were stored to be sold through the winter months. The price for late (main-crop) potatoes in the years before the war had only been from £1 to £2 per ton, which was a very depressed price and well below a reasonable return. In the winter after the War started that the price rose to around £5 per ton — much to Dad's relief. You may think this selfish, to be worrying about the price of potatoes at the start of the devastation of a world war, but for my Father having just doubled his size of farm, the price of each crop was the difference between success or failure. The challenge from the Country was to grow more food — for Dad the immediate challenge was to make his farm finances balance, or he and his family would have been on the road.

Most farmers were inspired by noble thoughts of what the Country required, but the real incentive to higher food production was the money each crop produced. I once asked Dad if he had been called up in the First World War, to which he replied to the effect that they didn't want us farm lads. It was only well after his death that I heard through the family of his boyhood friend, Tom Bell, that in fact they had both tried to enlist. They walked from their homes near Holmes Chapel with two or three other farm boys from the area to enlist in Chester. The queue was long at the recruitment office, and as the day wore on they did not seem to make any progress. Dad got impatient and bribed one of the supervising soldiers with a shilling and they moved up a bit, but it took two or three more shillings to get them as far as the medical. Eighteen year old farm boys were as fit as anyone, so they passed through with no problems and went into the last hurdle which was just to sign their names. The officer sat behind his desk and read their files. After a few minutes he looked up and said *"I think you boys will do a lot more for the war effort back home on your farms"*. They walked the 25 miles back to their farms, arriving back in the early hours of the next morning,, tired and dejected. When the Second World War came Dad was under no illusion as to what his role was, and he set out to produce the maximum possible — but always balancing the books whilst he did it!

The two Gough boys both volunteered for the army within a month of the start of the War. Jim was about twenty-seven and by then a very experienced timber man. He had spent many a long day swinging a seven-pound axe, so he had no trouble passing his medical. At the end he got that same message as Father in the First World War; his skills were of greater use to his country outside the army. He was to spend the war years felling timber for the war effort, to go where and when he was directed by the Ministry. On the other hand Geoff was only twenty, and although he had spent all his time working with Jim, he was accepted into the Army in November 1939. His enlistment was delayed for three months because his father was so desperately ill. After the death of his father in the early Spring of 1940, Geoff joined the 24th Medium, Royal Artillery Training Regiment in March 1940.

Harry Gough's funeral got a well deserved mention in the *Knutsford Guardian*, particularly because he had been a timber merchant of some renown. In his will he requested that his body should be carried to Lower Peover Church on his own timber waggon, and that it was to be pulled by his favourite horse Prince. That tall dark horse had killed a man, had been corrected so dramatically by Ned with a pick-axe handle, and had in turn grown in Harry Gough's affection to become his trusted friend. So trusted that Harry had no doubts about its behaviour even among a lot of people milling around at his own funeral. The horse was so much a friend that Harry wanted to know that he would be near him on his last journey.

That winter had been one of very heavy snow, with strong winds drifting it into the country lanes in a dramatic way. One of our buildings ran alongside the road and the warmth of the cattle in it melted the snow on the low roof. Icicles formed under the spouting, and after several snowfalls the icicles reached down to the footpath to create a spectacular ice wall that was photographed by many. Miss Webb, the junior teacher at Lower Peover, made it her duty to walk to every outlying home where there were children, to tell them not to come to school until the roads were cleared. It took two or three weeks to clear the lanes. I have often wondered how long it took Miss Webb to walk through snow drifts around the parishes of Lower Peover, Allostock, Plumley and Toft. Whilst at our farm she took her photo of the icicles and enjoyed showing it for some years afterwards.

Our farmhouse had a divided roof, with a gully between the new front part and the old at the rear. The lead channel in the bottom of that roof gully was only folded under the slates a few inches. When snow settled in the gully, the warmth of the house would melt it, but the snow still blocked the gully, so the water came over the lead. Harry's younger brother Eric had joined him on the staff just before we left Cheadle farm, and they shared a bedroom on the East side of our big

130

farmhouse. Several mornings they woke up to find two or three icicles hanging from their bedroom ceiling under the gully. There was only a fire in the kitchen, so the rest of the house was cold; so cold that we boys often found ice on the potties under our beds!

We children attended Sunday School at Ollerton Methodist Chapel, a walk of just over a mile. The lane was so full of snow we found it easier to walk in the fields on the east side of the lane just behind the hedge where the wind had blown the snow away. The drifts of snow were dramatic everywhere. Behind our farm the deep-sided brook in places was bridged over with snow, to the extent that it looked like a shallow hollow. After there had been a keen frost in the night, the snow had a hard crust that easily carried my young legs across its frozen surface. There was one length along the brook where the brook flowed through an old pond, and the west bank was very low. There the snow had created a long steep slope from the east that bridged across the brook. Because of the danger of falling through the snow into the frozen water below, I had been told to stay away from the brook; alas, I was not obedient and was busy developing a super slide down it when Dad caught me! I got a good walloping and was sent to bed without my tea.

For my first few months at Lower Peover school, Mother walked along with me, pushing her bicycle to ride it home, and in the afternoon she would return to guide me home again. My brothers had by then moved on to the Egerton School in Knutsford but my sister still went to Lower Peover so after a few months she

131

was entrusted with my safety. When I moaned about the walk to school, Dad told me it was only a mile and he had had to walk much further when he was a boy. My older brothers would join in with their condemnation of little boys who complained about a short walk. This year when I was writing this book I asked them both how far it was to school, they both said "about a mile". Well, I have now measured the distance and it was just under two miles, so I can only presume that each of them had in turn complained and Dad had told them the same answer, "*Well, it's only a mile, I walked a lot further when I was a boy*". In fact the old rogue didn't walk as far by a half mile!

The journey took us past the village green, across a field by the Smithy in dry weather or if wet we went round the lane, down Barrow Brow, over the Peover Eye and into Church Walk. There we passed Mrs Cragg's shop before crossing the graveyard to pass through the lychgate and down the cobbled stone lane to the infant school.

Miss Laurie was my teacher for the first year, and she had a stimulating way of teaching children to read. Each of us had to read to her two or three times each week; when it was my turn to stand by her desk, she sat by me with her hand behind my bare leg. If I couldn't say a word that she thought I should know, I got a slap behind my knee; the incentive was to guess but if I did and guessed wrong, I got two slaps. I am not sure that it helped me to read but it sure did improve my anticipation level!

The village was still a fascinating place to a small boy. Although the thrashing machines were no longer by the village green, it was a crossroads so they sometimes passed through when travelling from farm to farm. I loved to watch the steam engine belching smoke. The battener had been replaced by a large baler and both it and the thrashing box would trail behind the engine, all so large they filled the small lanes. It took two men to operate the engine on the road, one to steer, and the other in front of him to keep the steam up. Both of them were covered in soot and oil; it seemed that they were always squirting oil onto the brass bearings, then wiping their hands on an old rag — all the the rag achieved was a more even spread of the oil and grime. They could have walked onto the stage of a black and white minstrel show without make-up and looked the part.

The Peover Eye always held my attention. I remember clearly one occasion when Mum had to come back for me. I was just standing on the small bridge staring in to the water. What was I looking at? I don't know. Was it the movement, the reflection and light in the rippling water that held me or some genetic stirring in my little breast? Even now after so many years I can put down my fishing rod and just sit and watch that flowing, gurgling stream with the same dreamy fascination.

Mrs Cragg's little shop was full of goodies; she made her own humbug toffee, boiled in a large cast iron pan which hung from a blacksmith-made arm over her fire. It was a clever bit of engineering because not only could she swing the pan on and off her fire, the arm holding the pan could be adjusted for height as the fire burned down. Her humbug toffee brought people from afar and the fact that her shop was only a few yards from the Bells added to its appeal. Refined ladies could wander across the corner of the churchyard to indulge themselves to a quarter pound of Mrs Cragg's humbugs whilst their men folk drank another pint of Bell's beer.

Toffee was the only thing that I had on my mind as I passed the shop each day, but in fact she sold a whole range of food and household goods. Her pork and home-cured ham and bacon were of equal repute to the humbugs; not only home-cured but home-killed in the backyard right behind the shop. Mrs Cragg sold more than a pig every month. She had to kill each of them behind her shop and, being a small closely knit village, "pig killing day" was known in advance. When a boy at school before the War, Geoff Gough would slip away in his dinner hour to help the butcher. There was no humane killer in those days, so four people had to hang onto a leg each whilst the butcher slit the pig's throat. Mrs Cragg's pork pigs were not very large so a school boy could hold one leg, whilst the pig was held down on a small wooden curved cradle made for that job. It seems a hard way to die now that we have humane killers and electric stun guns, but even then an expert butcher made the death very quick for each pig. The dead pig was slid into a bath of near boiling water to soften the hair which could then be scraped off. Then the pig was hung to clean out the insides. Not much was wasted; heart, liver and kidneys were all sold

134

through the shop; even the intestines were used for sausage skins. A little later in the day two or three blood spattered small boys crept back into school with a cheeky grin on their faces.

I had strict orders that I was not to go near Arnold Jackson at the Smithy. Most mornings there were two or three horses there, occasionally more, waiting outside his smithy to be shod. It was obviously no place for small boys to be creeping around. We were brought up to stay well clear of working horses and distracted horses waiting at the Smithy were even more dangerous than alert working ones. Those horses knew what they were there for. Some of them just hated being shod and could get quite flighty whilst they were waiting. On the other hand there was always the old horse who had seen it all before, and balanced casually on three legs, just nodded off whilst waiting.

A trip to the Smithy was a social half day away from work for the waggoner; he had time to chat to others waiting with their horses, and meet people who were in the village on other business. Arnold stopped this by bringing in a rule that the farmers had to leave their horse at the Smithy, to be collected later that day after he had shod it. This got Father mad; he thought it was a complete waste of time. Often he would send two horses to be re-shod together and there was no way that Harry could push his bike with one hand and lead two horses with the other. If the road had been completely quiet it may have been possible but in those early years of the War there was more traffic — noisy, smoke belching motor lorries which could scare the most

135

placid horse. Harry was even less happy than Dad because he had to walk his horses to the Smithy, then return home to do some manual work, then walk back for his horses in the afternoon. When he arrived back at the farm it was too late to work them that day and Father would fume about a wasted half day.

I was with Dad at the Smithy when Arnold was trying to shoe one of those old relaxed giants. He lifted the horse's front foot, gripping the massive leg between his knees and he began to rasp away at the hard hoof. After a few moments the horse just slowly sagged down onto him, pressing him down with its great weight. I presume that it had actually gone to sleep. Arnold declared it was sleepy old horses like that one that ruined his back, but he slapped and shouted to no avail. Dad went and stood by the horse's head, but even then he had to keep digging it in the ribs with the butt end of his penknife to keep it awake. Dad couldn't resist making the point that had the waggoner been allowed to stay with the horse, he could have kept it awake. Arnold soon had enough of that argument and called a youth out from the deeper bowels of the Smithy. I was not sure if he was the next generation of the Jackson family or just an apprentice, but whichever, he took over from Dad and saved two short tempered men from blowing a fuse.

Arnold Jackson wouldn't change his rule for Dad. I think he just hated people standing around the Smithy watching him work. On the other hand, after I had been at school a couple of years I came along the footpath as he was about to hoop a wooden wheel (put an iron tyre or rim on). He took great care to explain (to what to him must have been an irksome small boy), each move of the task, and as the years went by I found that Arnold would always make time to explain his work to interested children.

It was all done outside, across the road from the green by a small pond that has now been filled in. Arnold had lit a fire of coal, logs and branches, so large that it had warmed the whole of the iron hoop evenly and when I got there it all glowed red with heat. The wooden wheel had been made by Peter Gough; it had an elm naive (centre) which had been turned to be perfectly symmetrical, oak spokes and ash fellows (outer rim). Ash is a more flexible wood so it was used to give the fellows a bit of spring. The wheelwright needed a lot of skill to make a wheel to match the other three on a lorry. Because each wheel leaned out from the lorry at an angle, the spokes were so butted in the naive that each spoke would be vertical as it touched the ground when the weight of the load would be on it. The iron tyre was also tapered to be flat on the road whilst the wheel was sloping well away from vertical. Those wooden wheels took an awful pounding; each joint had to be a perfect fit; any hint of looseness or filling, in any part of the wheel, would soon show up and bring an irate farmer to demand his money back.

Arnold had the wheel on an iron cradle which stood about two feet high. It was slightly dished toward a large hole in the centre, which allowed the naive to bulge through. It was designed to hold different sizes of wheels firm, whilst the iron tyre was put on. It took two men to lift the red hot tyre out of the fire and place it over the wooden rim of ash fellows. Flames and smoke billowed out as the iron was knocked down onto the wheel. When it settled flush with the edge of the fellows, water was immediately poured over it to both stop the hot iron burning the wood and to cool it, which made the iron shrink onto the wood. It was then I realised why it was all taking place by the pond, because it took several buckets of water to put out the flames and shrink the iron tyre. The end result was a tyre held by no more than its own contraction, held so firmly that it would stand years of pounding along rough gravel lanes and farm drives without working loose.

Miss Ellwood was the headmistress at our school. She was also sister to the vicar. To me as a child it didn't seem that she took any interest in the younger children, but I am sure that that was a false impression. She taught the seniors and whatever supervisory roll she may have had with us younger children, it did not seem to include speaking to us. Miss Webb on the other hand had the wonderful ability to make us all feel important. After Miss Laurie's leg slapping methods, Miss Webb seemed to be an angel of mercy, yet she still kept complete control of a mixed sex, mixed age group class. Phillip Harrop was a kindly man and as both school caretaker and church sexton I seemed to meet him a lot. It was a role that was easily combined as he could step over the separating stone flag fence between the playing field and the graveyard whenever he wanted to.

Mother would never admit that either Miss Webb or Phillip were related to her, but in fact they both fitted my Irish friends description by being "a sort of a cousin". Years later, after Phillip had tragically lost his first wife, he and Miss Webb married and enjoyed many happy years together. Miss Laurie was not in the first flush of youth but she had met a gentleman and they were looking desperately for somewhere to live after they were married. Houses were very scarce after the start of the War and their search proved fruitless. They eventually came to an agreement with my parents to erect a small secondhand sectional wooden bungalow at the end of our orchard. I can't remember much about them other than they seemed to be "very old". Her teaching methods didn't encourage me to go near them, and anyway, to my young mind, our orchard was really only a hen run and who would want to live in a hen run?

The War seemed a bit remote in those early months but after Dunkirk it became very real to everyone. My parents turned over part of our large farmhouse to two officers and their wives. Both had come back from Dunkirk in the spectacular evacuation and were glad of a quiet time to recoup both emotionally and physically. Time has erased one of their names from our memories but Captain Selkirk was with us the longest and made a lasting impression on we children. We became aware of what he had been through, and through him we knew of the horror and suffering of war.

I will always be grateful to Miss Webb's knowledge and love of the countryside, which she tried to impart to each of her children. Most weeks we were taken out down the cobbled stone lane for nature studies and when it was dry we would walk around the schoolfield. We boys were always fooling about, seemingly not paying any attention, but even so she managed to give me a lot of knowledge of wild flowers and plants. To aid the war effort, Miss Webb turned many of these outings into a foraging hour; we collected fruit and in particular rose hips. In fact anything to provide food or vitamin C. The operation was masterminded by the Women's Institute who collected every kind of fruit to bake, boil or make into jam. I once saw the record of the amount of jam and syrup that Lower Peover WI had produced through the War — it was a staggering achievement.

That walk to school past the village green brought my first contact with Jim Gough. He must have been taking a day off from his timber work when he saw a group of children on their way to school. The other children carried on walking but I stopped to answer the usual questions as he crouched down to ask them. "Who was I?" "How old?" "Did I like living at Toft etc?" I went on my way impressed that this tall muscular man should be interested in me and my life. Within a few weeks, his brother Geoff was home on leave and we met him taking a morning stroll along the lane. The same pleasant greeting to the group of us, followed by a sorting out of whose children we all were and how we were enjoying school, etc. I suppose if the same thing happened today it would be considered suspicious and they would both be carted off for questioning, but then it was part of village life to take

140

an interest in each family as they progressed through life. I have never forgotten their example of how important it is to speak to children, and more important, of how to speak without appearing condescending. From that time onwards, I held them in an awe and respect which has not diminished through the years.

CHAPTER EIGHT

The Trials of Buying a Horse

My older brothers found the woods on Toft estate fascinating places, the large mature trees dwarfed the blocks of rhododendron bushes and hidden among the trees were large ponds attracting many varieties of water birds. What was even more interesting to them was the timber felling taking place in the Windmill Wood. Jim Gough had been directed to provide timber for the War effort and it seemed natural to start in the woods he knew so well and where he knew there was mature timber waiting to be felled.

Arthur and George could walk across our fields and into the wood where Jim and his staff were felling tall scotch pine. The trunks when cleaned off were over a hundred feet long, so the height of the growing tree could have been nearer to 150 feet. Although Jim could usually fall a tree to which spot he choose, there was always a chance of one going wrong; because of that he made the boys stand well back.

The Goughs were using horses to both load and haul the timber. Perhaps once the loads were out on the road they were then pulled by a steam engine, but in the woods where the ground was soft it was horse power. Jim Gough made his own "three legs" out of three larch trees. Two were cut in to twenty feet lengths and the third was twenty-three feet long. The three poles were joined together at the top with a strong and long curved bolt through all three; the bolt was called a bow and the curve allowed the two shorter legs to splay out. All three poles were hooped at the top and bottom to prevent them from splitting, but the odd leg (tall pole) also had a sturdy metal peg driven some two feet up the centre from the bottom. This peg or dowel protruded over a foot and when sunk into the ground anchored the pole in place.

A treble pulley hung from the bow at the top and the rope came down from it to another one chained to the tree being loaded. The rope was usually threaded down and up two or even three times, but always coming through an additional snatch pulley fastened to the side of the actual tree being loaded; then finally through another pulley chained just above ground level on the odd leg. The reason for that was simply that a horse has more power if it is pulling slightly upwards. The harness on a horse would slip if the load was above the horse, but that bottom pulley gave the horse a stable weight low down which held the harness in place.

Heavy trees were not dangled clear of the ground but slid up two skids on to the timber waggon, which was parked under the three legs and parallel to the tree being loaded. Of course trees were not felled whilst others were being dragged out and loaded; horses however reliable, could not be worked with trees crashing to the ground around them, but over a few days it was possible to see all sides of the timber felling business.

On one of these adventures through the woods my brothers found a small rough coated terrier. There was no one about to claim it and the dog would not leave them, so they brought it home. We never did find out where it came from, but by how hungry it was, there seemed no doubt it was a stray. Arthur named her Judy and they became inseparable pals, both game for anything. Around the farm buildings we had a constant battle to keep rat numbers under control, and Judy joined in this battle with great enthusiasm. In winter when the stock was inside, each night at bedtime someone checked round the cattle, looking in to every shippen and loose box. There was seldom a night without Judy catching a rat or at least giving one or two a good chase. In fact we had such fun with her that there was plenty of volunteers to "look up" each night. Judy soon got to know our cats but she did not like strays — any visiting tomcat was fair game, and more than one came to a sad end on a dark winter's night.

Judy had one very bad fault in that she treated hedgehogs as though they were rats. Rolling into a ball was no protection for them; Judy just ripped them to pieces. In winter when they were seemingly safely hibernated, often down an old rabbit hole or perhaps under the roots of a tree, she would smell where they lay hidden, snug and asleep, dig them out and kill them in seconds. Arthur never managed to cure her of that one bad habit and always had to be alert to protect our hedgehogs. George had a smooth coated collie called Fido, who was equally ready for any fun that could be thought up. If Judy went into a briar bush after a rabbit, Fido waited alert on the outside, ready to give chase when it bolted.

Father persisted with his hens out in the fields; the hencote usually stood in the middle of the field in the hope that all the hens would be safely inside before it was dark enough for the fox to be about. Had the hencote been by a hedge a fox could creep along in its shadow in early dusk and take the odd hen before their bedtime. Even in the middle of the field each hencote had to be shut immediately after the last hen had gone into roost, because by then it was so near to dark that a bold fox would be on the prowl and would risk crossing the open field. One heavy snow fall came in the late afternoon, and many of the hens took shelter under a thorn hedge along one side of the field rather than go back to their cote. The snow was soon five or six inches deep and as the hens were reluctant to walk in that depth of snow, they chose to stay hidden under the low snow covered branches of the thick hawthorn hedge. It was nearly dark before my brothers realised there was a problem, but Fido found every hen, nosed them out from under the thorns and helped to drive them back to the hencote. Without her, most of them would have been slaughtered by foxes before morning.

Both those dogs slept in our large kitchen, Judy in a box in the corner and Fido on an old rocking chair. It was much too small for her but she would sleep nowhere else. My brothers roamed the fields and woods with those two dogs, but usually without me — they said I was too young or I couldn't keep up, or some other ridiculous excuse. I was left to follow Dad on his walks around the farm, when he would be looking round stock or taking baggin to his workers. He never had a good word to say about school but he sure set about educating me on those long walks. The farm was long and narrow, interspersed with mature woodland, a mile to the bottom and three quarters to the top. I had to learn to recognise each variety of tree on the way. Not just when they were in leaf but in winter when there was just an outline of shape. He would suddenly ask "What's that tree there?" There were still some red squirrels in the woods when we first went to Toft. I loved to watch them in the trees, or find their hidden store of hazel nuts. If Dad saw me poking under the roots of a tree he would suddenly say, "Don't look up, what tree is it?" I learned to recognise each type of tree by just looking at its bark. The red squirrels did not last long; one morning on our way to Sunday School we saw our last red squirrel being chased through the tree tops by three or four grey ones.

Experts tell us that grey squirrels do not kill red ones; well, I don't believe them. Even if they do not actually kill by attacking, they kill by harassment. Particularly in winter when the reds need to hibernate, the active greys force them out of their warm drays into certain death in the cold. One sad side effect is that I never see mature hazel nuts hanging on the bushes now, this is because grey squirrels eat them well before

146

they are ripe. The reds waited until the nuts were mature before harvesting them. They bit the nuts of the bushes, then carried them to selected hiding places, usually under the roots of large trees. Red squirrels would beaver away for hours filling their small stores with both hazel nuts and acorns. Grey squirrels also store acorns but they just bury individual ones randomly in the hope that they will find some in the winter.

For about eight weeks before calving again, in-calf cows take a rest from milking. During that time those "dry cows" have no need to come into the shippen each day, so they are usually put to graze the pastures furthest away from the buildings. At Toft this was the forty-acre meadow almost surrounded by woodland. The majority of our herd calved through September and October. It meant that in July and August and early September most of our cows were resting. This gave Father and his workers more time to harvest the cereals and potatoes, without spending too much time with the dairy herd. Unfortunately that is the time of year when dry cows can catch summer mastitis or what we called "August Bag". It is now accepted that the infection is carried by flies, and because there were plenty of those around our woods we had more than our share of the disease.

Through those two worst months (mid-July to mid-September), Dad looked at his dry cows twice each day. As it was also my school holidays I would often trot along with him. He would always stand at the gate and watch them for a few minutes, before walking round the field to count and inspect each cow. As he stood by the gate he could often spot a cow that was starting with August Bag just by the way it stood or acted; close inspection would usually prove him right, sometimes even before the udder was inflamed or swollen.

Not only did I learn to recognise those symptoms at an early age I learned to count. I really did! Every time I had to count those cows, if I didn't get them right I had to count again and again until my numbers matched Dad's. Even today in my retirement if we stop for a picnic along the roadside where there are cattle or sheep near, after a few minutes Celia will ask with a smile, "How many are there?" Because she knows that the habit of counting stock is so engrained in me that I will have made a count if only an approximate one.

Dad was not so attentive a stock looker through the rest of the year; he had the bad habit of leaving his check round until later in the day. Sometimes the demands of the business meant that he did not get round the stock until after work. Occasionally he missed going altogether and on one of those occasions, a strong colt had pushed through the fence. It was a lovely bay colt nearly three years old and out of a good working mare. Dad had bought it at a nearby farm dispersal sale intending that Harry should break it in the following summer, at three and a half years of age. Alas, the young horse went in to one of those peaty brooks which had no solid bottom, and sank until it drowned.

There were also two younger colts growing up out of Jewel. The oldest called Blue, a lovely light blue colour,

148

would be another year before she was ready to start work. Although Dad must have used a blue stallion on Jewel at Cheadle Farm to sire that one, the next colt Bonny was by a different stallion. Mr Robinson had retired when Dad came to this farm but he offered to help with the ploughing; this meant that Father needed another good plough horse. Three horses with the wide plough could plough one and a quarter acres each day but four horses in two teams with two men and two ploughs could plough two acres each day. Dad had the ploughs and he had the men so all he needed was another good steady horse. He realised that Jewel was nearing the end of her breeding age so he decided to buy a fully trained mare which could plough through the winter and hopefully then be served in the following spring.

I went with him to Crewe cattle market where they held a monthly horse sale and I was amazed at the numbers of people there. I believe there was about sixty horses on sale but Dad estimated there would about three hundred or more people attending. A bewildering mixture of people from smartly dressed farmers to others very much in their working clothes. A coloured hanky used as a neck-tie, knotted at the front, seemed to identify shifty looking horse dealers, whilst buyers from city organisations were recognisable by their pale faces and smooth skinned hands. Each town and city had a large number of heavy horses in haulage transport; the railways, breweries, feed merchants, even furniture removers, to name but a few, all relied on the heavy horse for power. Most of them bought their replacement horses at these type of auctions, when the horse was reaching its peak at about five years of age.

Farmers were the main suppliers, breaking in the colts at three and a half years of age, working them on light duty for the next year and bringing them up to full potential when they were about five years old. In fact Dad had one such colt on our farm, and he and Harry had broken it in that Autumn, but it would be another two years before it was ready for the hard slog of ploughing every day, for six days each week.

At the peak of horse power it was estimated there was more than a quarter of a million horses in London alone. Although perhaps less than a third of them were heavy horses, if you multiply that number for every city and town in the Country, the total number of heavy horses would have be enormous. You can then understand why the demand for sound well broken young horses had in the past been exceptional. Of course at the time of this sale in the early years of the War, motor lorries had replaced the heavy horse in many businesses, but the demand was still good. A three year old colt was worth about twenty five to thirty guineas, whereas a fully broken, well-trained five-year old could be worth three times that.

The sale ring was shaped like a key hole with the auctioneer at the top, and the horse was lead down the long straight length of the keyhole. This was achieved by both horseman and horse running at a fast trot for all to see its movements. Buyers were standing around the ring and down each side of the exercise area, two or three deep. Behind them on all sides were five or six levels of terraced planks for seats. The auctioneer had a couple of assistants to take the bids from among the packed buyers along each side of the exercise area. Farmers hated to let their neighbours see them bidding so, as the main auctioneer rattled away, always in guineas, his assistants standing along the exercise areas would be shouting "Yes" or "Here" and pointing into the crowed where a flick of a thumb or a wink had signalled a bid.

If the horse had not reached its reserve price, the auctioneer would say "Let it run again — look at that movement — did you ever see better?" Then he would rattle off again whether he had a bid or not, in the hope that he could attract another genuine bid. If he did not get a bid he would still pretend he had until he was well past the reserve price. He would then say, "Sorry Gentlemen, we can't go at that."

We sat high up, about half way along one side, with a good view of the whole ring. When the auctioneer let one horse run again, as its handler ran with it at full trot, a farmer just to the left of us poked it in the ribs with his cane. The massive shire shied and slipped, falling heavily, trapping his handler under its head and breaking the unfortunate man's arm. The auction stopped while people rushed to help. I added my pennyworth by saying in a loud voice "That man there poked it with his stick! That man there poked . . ." Dad got me away from there quick before I got him into a fight. Needless to say we didn't buy a horse.

The Sidar Field was the second field down across the road. It was long and narrow with woods down one side and across the bottom. The cow lane to the big meadow ran down the side, between the field and the Spinney Wood, then between the Mossynook Wood and a neighbour's field before reaching our forty-acre meadow. One or two sweet chestnut trees and the odd horse chestnut hung over the cow lane and gave an added attraction to my walks with Dad. I never knew the origin of the field name, perhaps at some time there had been a cedar tree there and the name had got corrupted to Sidar. The field rose to a hump in the middle and the soil type on that one field was a medium loam. It was completely different to anywhere else on the farm, and although it could be harder to work into a seed-bed, it grew exceptional crops. Dad liked to have that field ploughed first, allowing the winter frosts to work their magic on the heavier soil.

Harry was ploughing the Sidar with his team of three when a shooting party came on to it. He had ploughed over the hump when he heard several shots behind him. A covey of partridge came low over the hill, as they passed just in front of his team one partridge just folded its wings and dropped dead. He ploughed right past where it lay, casually picked it up as he passed and put it into his tweed jacket pocket. He worked on gripping the plough handles and reins in each hand. In the corner of his eye he noticed the under-keeper walking across the field, and then stand watching him. Harry was puzzled so he looked behind him — a big retriever was following him with its nose in the air, and it was pointing right at his pocket. He ploughed on regardless!

That under-keeper had a dreadful experience with poachers later that same winter. He had gone out in the night on his own to watch for poachers, and in fact caught up with some. Unfortunately they over-powered him and beat him up quite badly, then pushed him face down, head first into a large rabbit hole. They then drove a fencing stake into the ground between his legs, not very gently either. His wife had no idea which wood he had gone to, she only knew he had not returned by morning. She raised the alarm and the estate staff began to search but it was late in the day before he was found, and by then he was so near to death that his life hung in the balance for several hours. One can only imagine the horror of his plight, if he struggled soil would start to trickle down round his face and would have smothered him had he continued. Fastened so brutally he could only wait and hope for rescue, which was almost too late to save him. Even then the mental scars must have been enormous. He would need a lot of courage to venture out again in to those dark, menacing woods. If he regained his nerve I doubt if his wife could have stood the strain, and they resolved it by becoming the landlords of the old George and Dragon in Holmes Chapel.

The ploughing progressed from the Sidar Field to the long Twenty Acre behind the the Oak Wood, but still only Harry with his team of three. Late one afternoon the gentry took a hand again, but this time it was the hunt. The keeper had in the past given Harry a warning if the hounds were likely to come his way, but this time perhaps because he was recovering from the assault on him, no warning came. Harry was striding along behind the plough unaware that the hounds were about, when suddenly both hounds and horses galloped up behind him. As they passed him both Captain and Prince would have gone with them but for Jewel, and even Jewel had a little skip and jump. Harry ran to their heads and managed to get a grip on their bridles, but by then they were sideways to the ploughing. The horses had two or three feet on the wrong side of their chains. He had great difficulty in keeping control of his three horses. Even when the hunt had left the field it was some time before he dare let loose of their bridles to sort out their feet from the chains.

In those days the hunt kept on until dusk, particularly if the hounds were on cry. With so many woods both in and around the farm you never knew where they would chase a fox to. It was impossible to check every gate and fence after each hunt, particularly if there had been no warning that they were even crossing our farm. On one of those occasions the hunt had chased a fox across the top of the farm late in the day. Dad knew nothing about it until the next morning, when he found a gate left open and some young heifers in the Windmill Wood. There were yew trees in most of the woods and that wood had a row of yews down one side. The young green leaves are a deadly poison if eaten. Two heifers were already dead; two more died the next day. Several weeks later two more became ill on different days; the poison seemed to have affected their brains, causing them to lose orientation until they just walked round in circles. I watched one from the safety of the garden; it was walking the same path round and round until the grass was churned into mud. It took three men with ropes and brute force to load it into a lorry so that it could be transported away for slaughter. Father never forgave the hunt, it seemed to affect him deeply, to the extent that he was nearly paranoid in his hatred of red jackets and horses ever after.

That day Dad and a couple of men drove down to the wood and loaded the two dead heifers in to the cattle trailer he still shared with John Clarkson. As he knew John wanted it the next day, he and Harry went off to Donkey Warberton's knacker's yard with the dead beasts that evening. It was Harry's first visit to that yard near to Altrincham and it came as quite a shock to him; he was unprepared for the smell and sight of an old style knacker's yard. Donkey Warberton got his name from hiring out two or three donkeys to fun days, or garden parties. The donkeys would go anywhere that the organisers could charge children a few pence for a ride, but of course Donkey had a draw out of it. He also dealt in all sorts of horses, not just heavy shire types, but what we called "half-legged" ones, often a cross between a shire and a riding horse. The result was literally seen in the legs, which were stronger than a riding horse's but without the feathering (long hair) on the legs that marked a good heavy horse. That type was often used on milk rounds or on similar work where brute strength was not so important. The smaller horse ate less food and the fact that they could often trot (which a heavy shire found tiring) speeded up light

155

delivery work. Just as there are van hire people today, then Donkey hired any of his horses out for a day or a week or whatever. In fact he would hire or sell you any type of horse or horse harness you might require.

It was after tea by the time Harry and Dad got to the yard, and at first they could find no one to say where to put the dead heifers, so they took the chance to have a good look around. There were six cast iron boilers bubbling away, each cooking meat to supply a contract with Belle Vue Zoo in Manchester. A mixture of all types of horses were housed in a large loose-boxes, with a few heavy shires in a separate one. In another building two or three old and decrepit cows lay on a bit of straw, moaning and groaning in their pain and discomfort as they waited to be slaughtered the next day. To add to the colour of the scene, at the back of the yard a pile of dismembered bodies were piled by the wall, waiting to go into the boilers.

An old woman came out of the house and indicated to them where to put the carcasses which by this time were terribly bloated with gas. She plunged a large carving knife in to each stomach, completely oblivious to the released gas that exploded all over her. On other occasions callers had often commented how they had seen her sitting on a carcass, knife in hand, unconcerned at the unconventional place to take a rest. I believe that Donkey Warberton's wife lived on their farm at Plumley, so there was a bit of speculation as to his relationship to the woman at the knacker's yard.

The story was told how one farmer, who had called at the knacker's yard to buy some secondhand horse

156

harness, had been invited by Donkey to join him for his mid-day meal. The farmer found it very appetising and as they walked across the yard afterwards, he felt obliged to tell Donkey just how good his dinner had been. Donkey replied "Yes, it was an old sow that came in last week, I though it too good to waste." The farmer ungratefully brought it all up again in the middle of the yard, right at Donkey's feet.

Father must have indicated when he and Harry were at the knacker's yard, that he needed another working horse urgently. Within a day or two Donkey Warberton brought him a good looking mare to try. Dad agreed, but strictly on the understanding that it was on trial and could be returned if it didn't measure up. With many town businesses changing to motor transport there was a reverse trade in horses. Many farm bred horses were becoming redundant in towns and were going back to the land to help the drive for more food. This mare seemed to fit into that category and for a few weeks ploughed with a will. Well, she did until she came to a muddy area. Autumn ploughing had to go on through quite wet weather, the horses may stay in the stable on very wet days, but would be out again the day after the rain had stopped. After heavy rain it could be very soft under foot, and even squelchy in places. Harry found that his new mare did not like the soft ground at all. She must have been a town-bred horse that had always worked on hard roads. With no experience of soft ground she just refused to pull the plough through any soft or muddy patch.

157

Donkey exchanged her for another ex-city mare, but this one would work on soft ground and seemed the perfect mare for our needs. After she had been with us for a couple of months Dad was in the farm house enjoying a cup of tea, when Harry called him out. I was on holiday from school so I trotted along to see what was going on. As Dad strode out into the yard, Harry explained to Dad that the horse was a "shiverer" and would not back a load into the dutch barn. Apparently if a horse's back had been injured — perhaps it had slipped when pulling a heavy cart load or it had even just been over-loaded enough to damage its back — such an injury may not show up until that horse was asked to push a heavy load backwards. It needed a completely different set of muscles to reverse a heavy load, so when this mare was asked to back she started trembling with anticipation of the pain, hence the horse term "shiverer".

Mum came out to make sure that I was out of the way, explaining that no one could know what an unproven horse might do in those circumstances. I stood by the wall as Dad tried to make the mare push the cart load of straw back into the barn. She became wild eyed and was obviously in distress, even so the mare did make two attempts to push backwards but the pain must have been too much for her. Father was not amused. He had a good rant about horse dealers messing him about and seemed to be in the mood to blame Harry and anyone else standing near. When Warberton's man came to collect the horse a few days later it was working in the field, the man slipped

158

something out of his pocket and into the horse's mouth. Harry claims that most horse dealers had a magic potion that would both quieten a horse and dull any pain; it was given to this one so that it could be taken to the next customer and put through its paces without showing any distress.

Dick Willet lived on a small farm about a mile from us and nearer to Knutsford. He was a noted character, in fact there is a now restaurant where his farm stood, which is named after him. He milked a few cows and sold the milk on a small milk round on the edge of Knutsford. Setting out after breakfast with the milk in a carrier on the front of a strongly built push bike, he would make the deliveries last until noon. His final delivery was to the Paradise Garage about a half mile from his home, where he would fill in any surplus time before noon with a cup of tea, taken in winter next to the old oil burning heater.

At certain times in the year Dick Willet's own cows would not produce enough milk to supply his customers so Dad sold him (illegally because it was against the MMB rules) a few gallons of milk each day. This trade between them laid out in my Father's records show the more relaxed way of life then, by the fact that Dad sent a bill once a year in December and one year it hadn't been paid so he sent a reminder — the following December. I should add that there were several different deals back and to between the two; the bill which was the difference over the whole year did not amount to much and could easily have been overlooked.

Dick Willet helped to supplement the income from his small farm by breaking in colts for other farmers. Occasionally he trained one of his own which he would then sell. One of those, a young mare, he persuaded Dad to buy. Judy was what Dad called "a short-coupled horse", which was his way of describing a strong but short-bodied horse. The mare had not got the full feathered legs of a shire but had a little more than one would expect on a Suffolk. I can only presume she was a cross between the two breeds.

Dad both worked her and bred from her for many years, but like many horses she had a fault. Judy worked with a will, either on her own or in harness with another and Harry was very pleased with her until a few days of wet weather stopped the field work. The horses had been kept on their working diet with the intention of working the next day, only to be rained off again, and again. When finally the rain stopped and Harry took his team out on the land, they were "steamed up" and raring to go, but after about an hour Judy just stopped and refused to move. A horse that jibs is the most frustrating beast and of no use to anyone. But Judy was not really a "jibber" and after a frustrating hour she proved it by working on for weeks without a problem.

Harry had begun to think that the incident was a complete fluke when the same circumstances were repeated. Three days of rain had finally ended, the sun shone, Judy was over-fit and by mid-afternoon the soil was dry enough to go on a worked field with the flat roller. Judy worked for about an hour and then just

160

stopped; Harry tried hard to make her move, but each time she just ran backwards. We were on holiday from school and my sister Mary had been sent out with Harry's baggin, and she came back with the report that Judy had jibbed. Dad wouldn't let me go with him, but strode off in not the best of a mood. I don't know what he did to get Judy moving again; I do know it was about an hour before he returned and when I saw the field afterwards it looked like a lounge wall that had had a paint roller stroked playfully across it. Each time they had tried to start Judy she had run backwards in the shafts of the roller, pushing it in a curving thirty yard run, first one way and then the other in a series of sweeps that took them across the field.

Again after that incident Judy worked on for many weeks before the same set of circumstances created the same result, and that fault remained with her throughout her life. On one occasion Harry had gone to collect some oats from Holford Mill when Judy stalled on the way home. He didn't waste time trying to move her; he tied the reins to the fence and walked home for his faithful Jewel. When he returned Judy was still in the same spot so he just hitched Jewel in front of her and when Jewel pulled she either had to walk or be dragged. Needless to say she walked home as though nothing had happened. Dad didn't blame Dick Willet for the horse's fault; he accepted that it was one of those things that Dick could not have known about. Once they got to know what might trigger it off, it could usually be avoided by cutting out Judy's oats at slack times, or by turning her into the field on rest days.

CHAPTER
NINE

The Need for More Food

The German U-boat packs were making a dramatic in-road into our imports; none more so than our food supplies. I seem to remember Winston Churchill condemning the British position in the strongest of words, in that as a nation we had been happy to rely so much on imported food. Before the War we had been a manufacturing nation, dependent on our export of goods. Poor countries who needed our manufactured goods often had no money but usually had cheap labour and good land. We British became dependent on that cheap source of food, developing a variety of complex barter deals to exchange food for our exports. The food was cheap but the price was high; at the start of the war we scarcely produced 40% of the food we needed. Our own agriculture had stagnated, some farms stood empty and unoccupied and on those that were farmed, investment was almost non-existent — whilst abroad, the so called cheap food was often produced by exploitation and in some countries even slavery.

To be fair the Government had realised the danger and had tried to give farming a kick start in the mid-1930s. Those farmers who had managed to live through the Depression had done so by caution, so a few subsidies or encouraging words were not going to make them bold. Father's pet saying was "The Banks will lend you an umbrella when the sun shines, but ask for it back when it rains". Needless to say, he did not like to borrow money and yet, he was without doubt one of the more dynamic of farmers.

The Government decided that an increase in food production could not wait for the cautious response from farmers, so they formed a War Agriculture Executive Committee, known to all as the "War Ag". Below the National Committee there was one for each County who in turn supervised local War Ag Committees, which were made up mainly of retired or semi-retired people. They ranged from civil servants who had a bit of an agricultural background, to returned colonels, with a few ageing farmers added in to give them a practical face. Between them they packed enormous power over farmers; each farm was visited and studied. Pressure was put on every farmer to grow crops rather than grass. Old turfs had to be ploughed and brought into a rotation; even park land around many of the old country houses was ploughed for the first time in living memory.

Many farmers were not equipped, either with machinery and finance, or even mentally, to respond to the drive for food. The Government responded by bringing in American machinery and providing loans to enable farmers to buy it. They provided advice for those who wanted to respond but lacked the experience and if all else failed the War Ag had the power to take over the farm. Dad never spoke very respectfully about our local War Ag, he felt they were a ineffective bunch without the practical knowledge needed. On the other hand they respected him because he was doing all the things they required. He ploughed out the old pastures, releasing their store of fertility in to a crop rotation; he increased his potatoes to around thirty acres per year; he maximised their production with the careful use of cow muck; and of course there was the second crop of cabbage or winter greens grown with the early potatoes.

In the early years of the War, Dad kept his dairy herd numbers static at about forty. I believe there was a scheme to reduce them in some parts. Because of Dad's arable production his dairy numbers were accepted but he gave up rearing heifers and came to rely on bought dairy cows. Although I am sure he did respond to the call for more food, I am equally sure that his response was carefully calculated as to what would pay. There was no way that Dad could have been made to grow a crop that may not have paid. At the same time he used to laugh about other farmers who would not respond to the War Ag's exhortations. The "Agricultural Return" entered into the farming vocabulary — it was a form to be filled in by each farmer, showing crops, grass and stock numbers. His return for June 1941 was as follows:

Oats	33 acres	Milking cows	38
mixed corn with wheat	10 acres	Dry cows	3
mixed corn no wheat	13 acres	bulls	1
early potatoes	7 acres	bull calves	1
late potatoes	14 acres	youngstock	
swedes	½ acre	under two years	14
Mangolds	2½ acres	under one year	3
mowing	31 acreas	killing calf	1
pasture	54 acreas	pigs	3
total	165 acres	horses — heavy geldings	2
		mares	2
		others such as unbroken colts and foals	5

250 fowl, 30 ducks and 8 geese completed the list.

Inspectors would come to check that you were doing what you said you were, or had in fact grown the potato acreage that you were instructed to. Unfortunately the inspectors themselves were not always the most competent of people. Dad loved to tell about one farmer who had neither the ability or the intention to grow his allotted acreage of potatoes. Instead of the twenty acres that he was supposed to grow, he put in just nine on one field but in his returns claimed to have grown another eleven acres further down his farm. Of course he was inspected, but unabashed he took the inspector to the near end of the nine acres. Then on a circular route that took them around a small wood, and along the back of some overgrown and dense thorn hedges, he eventually arrived at the other end of the same field and pursuaded the Inspector that it was the other eleven acres.

There were many capable people serving their Country by working for the War Ag, but the other type were the ones who got talked about. That is best illustrated by Dad's request to buy a new corn drill nearer the end of the war. New machinery could only be bought with a permit which was usually granted after an inspection to see that the old machine was indeed worn out. In this case the drill was fairly good but Dad wanted a larger one. The inspector arrived whilst Dad was having breakfast and he did not like to be disturbed during that meal. It was always Mum who had to leave her breakfast to answer the door. She gave the inspector directions as to where the old corn drill stood behind the hay shed, then added that Father would be out in a few minutes.

When Dad went out he found the confused man walking round a very decrepit cultivator that stood forlorn and neglected in a bog of nettles. The only semblance to a corn drill was the fact that it had two wheels, other than that it was just a crude cultivator that Dad had bought cheap at a farm sale, hoping that it could be used to cultivate his Autumn stubble. It proved to be no good for that purpose and was just left to rust away, unloved and forgotten until that inspector decided that it definitely needed replacing with a new corn drill. To be fair to Father, he didn't pretend that it was a corndrill, he just stood well back and let the Ministry man walk to him with the good news. Dad became quite attached to it after that and loved to take visitors to see it and tell the story.

The men from the Ministry really ruled our lives. There were also inspections for rabbit control, rat control and of course constant rules and inspection over the production and sale of the foods on ration. Perhaps one of the worst for Dad to comply with was the control of rabbits. Toft woods were full of deep warrens and at dusk the wood side fields literally swarmed with hundreds of rabbits. The growing crops of cereals would be eaten down for a strip some twenty or thirty yards wide along the side of each of the woods. Both Harry and Eric spent their spare time "rabbiting" — perhaps of the two Eric was the keener shot. He still remembers how, when he crept up to a field to shoot one rabbit, the whole field side seemed to move as the rest ran for safety.

The War Ag instructed Dad to erect wire netting along the worst lengths to try to protect the young crops. To stop them burrowing under the wire he ploughed out a furrow and stood the netting in the bottom, then pushed back the soil; even then a few managed to dig under. A surprising number of rabbits found their way round the netting, or perhaps they came across the field from the many warrens along each of the other hedges. Whatever the reason, they were then on the wrong side the wire the next morning. I think Dad deliberately erected the wire on a Friday when we kids would be at home the following morning, or even better when perhaps we were on holiday. Early the following morning we would be off with Fido the collie and armed with short curved sticks to do battle. Judy was banned from this sport because rabbits were worth money and if Judy caught one it was worth nothing — in fact if you did not get it away from her quickly it didn't even look like a rabbit.

Most of the rabbits trapped behind the fence lay "clapped" (lying flat with ears down) out in the crop, so we walked abreast parallel to the wood. Fido was often the first to put one up and then the chase was on. She very seldom caught a rabbit but she stayed right behind them, twisting and turning at full speed to every evasive dodge of the rabbit until they both hit the fence. By then we would have been at the fence, one at either side, and whether the bunny broke left or right, with luck one of us would sweep sideways with our short curved stick. In reality it was not that simple, many rabbits had an incredible ability to dodge both small boys, dogs and wire netting, but it was seldom that one ran across the open field to the safety of the far hedge.

It may seem cruel sport now, but then the Country was desperate for food and in fact we were compelled to use every possible means to control the vermin. Ministry-supplied shotgun cartridge were issued in white cases; Harry and Eric used a lot of them on summer nights when stalking the feeding bunnies, but they were not impressed by those wartime-produced cartridges. Dad bought the cartridges but he had the rabbits that the two brothers shot, selling most of them to passing lorry drivers, who in turn sold them in their home towns.

You would think that with all those rabbits the foxes would have had plenty of food without bothering our hens. Not so, Reynard could not resist a chicken, nor for that matter could he resist a go at a mass slaughter if given a chance. The hens were free range and on some occasions a fox would come whilst everyone was having their midday meal. Dad used to say they must have a watch, but in reality the fox would just creep along the side of the deep brook and wait until all was quiet, then a quick dash into the farm yard to nip of a few heads before carrying one away to eat later.

In the evening twilight foxes would come out onto the fields to play about. We often watched them rolling and tumbling, or chasing each other in mock fights. They liked to catch moths which they "nosed" out of the bogs of grass growing around cow pats, leaping high to snap them in mid-air. Even when the foxes were so occupied they were still alert and it was hard to get near them. Eric developed a method of stalking foxes that he still loves to talk about. He would select a quiet old cow and drive it towards the fox, keeping low so that his outline was not seen either above or to the side of the cow. He kept herding her along until he got in range; many times he shot a fox over the cow's back.

In the dark winter nights there was no chance to walk the fields with a gun, so the brothers used a "long net" to catch rabbits. When the two of them went together they used about three nets of some sixty yards each in length. Sometimes when Dad was with them they would use over two hundred yards of nets, sometimes taking fifty or sixty rabbits at one setting. If stretched wide the nets would have been three to four foot high, but when erected were only about twenty seven inches high, leaving plenty of loose netting to entangle the rabbits. There was a foot-long anchor peg at both ends of each net; tied to it were two cords running top and bottom for the whole length of each net. To carry nets with out them getting tangled, each was carefully looped onto one anchor peg whilst the second was tied round to secure the net.

To erect the net, one man heeled in the anchor peg, just by pressure, no stamping or foot falls or every rabbit would hear and be back home before the net was erected. The same man would then walk quietly in a straight line, keeping about twenty or thirty yards out from the wood side to avoid getting twigs in the nets. Skill was needed to let the net run through his hands and off the other end peg without getting in a tangle. The second man followed behind erecting the net, using touch to loop the top cord round each hazel peg which he pushed into the ground every five to seven yards. This was all done in complete silence and always on a dark windy night, with no moon to light their way. They never even carried a torch, and a moonlit night was avoided because it would have let the rabbits see the nets. A wind was necessary to take their smell and what noise they made away from the feeding rabbits. So wind direction dictated where they could set their nets and even how they approached the chosen site, but it sometimes brought others to the same place on the same night. Knowing what had happened to the underkeeper, Harry never walked along the side of a

170

hedge, or fence or under trees; in fact anywhere that someone could wait concealed was treated with caution. On a few occasions they had walked quietly to their chosen site to find other poachers there before them.

Once they stood hidden in the shadows whilst our neighbour's two sons netted a length of our field. Rabbits could be feeding two fields away so in a case like that it would be a long walk round to the back of the rabbit's feeding area. The poachers running the rabbits in would have to walk parallel with the nets, to and fro to sweep the rabbits in towards the nets. Most poachers coming onto another gang like that would have crept out whilst they were away, taking what rabbits they could before cutting the net cords; but the Davies boys did not want to start a feud. There was no law out in among the fields and woods on those pitch black winter nights, every man looked out for himself. When Dad was netting he always had one person stay with the nets to guard them; it had been known for one gang of poachers to steel another's nets.

The Davies brothers were not poaching when they were on our land, but gamekeepers did not approve of farm lads netting rabbits. Most keepers had an arrangement or even worked with a rabbiting gang, as long as the poachers left the pheasants and partridge alone. The keeper then turned a blind eye to their rabbiting, and discouraged the farm boys from netting. On the other hand the Davies brothers were not too fussed which side of the boundary fence they set their nets. As they went about their farm work they saw

171

which crops the rabbits were travelling to, and when the wind was in the right direction they would have a go at whichever side of the fence was best. They set their nets on one occasion on the neighbour's field and right behind the keeper's cottage garden. To their dismay they caught a large wild tomcat in the net and he was a fearful animal, leaping, twisting and slashing with his claws as he tried to get free of the entangling net. Had the keeper walked down the garden path to his ivy-clad privy he would have heard the most frightful row. There was no chance of freeing the hissing, spitting, snarling cat in the dark so alas he had to be "quietened" quickly.

The two boys were not encouraged to "join up". In fact they were positively discouraged; their skills were needed to feed the nation. At the same time they were expected to enlist in the Home Guard when they were old enough. First Harry and then later Eric, when he became eighteen, joined in what was to them a quite boring force. Most of their time was spent guarding their own HQ which was a large house on the outskirts of Knutsford. One night each week was spent on this guard duty. The plan was to do two hours on duty, then have four hours sleep before going back on duty again. The reality was that they all slept in one large room, so by the time that two guards had noisily got dressed to go on duty and then the two guards coming off duty had finally got into bed, there wasn't much of the four hours left to sleep.

Harry was sent on an exercise to cross Tabley Park on a dark and windy night; just the kind of night for long-netting rabbits. He was fairly confident of his ability in our own fields in the dark, but he found the strange surroundings an absolute nightmare; he thought that he would never make it to the other side to "capture" an old barn. On the other hand their shooting skills were soon tested out. Eric particularly proved his worth when he was taken one Saturday to a shooting ground. The constant use of a shotgun in summer and a air-gun for shooting rats in winter had developed his natural ability. He felt confident with a .22 rifle in his hands and was proud that a penny could cover the four holes his first four shots made in the target.

Even in the Home Guard the farmer's crops took priority, and they were excused duty if they were needed on the farm. There was never any argument if Dad was harvesting or needed them to work overtime for any other reason, Dad took priority. It is hard to realise just how desperately the country needed to increase food production. From a production base of less than 40% before the war we had to grow food to replace those lost imports or be starved into submission. Even when the boys had done a night on duty at their HQ they left in the morning at 5.30 to be back at the farm in time to start work at six.

After 1941 most of the cereal crops that Dad grew were a mixture of wheat, oats and barley to provide better cattle feed. Although sown together in Spring they did not ripen at the same time. The unripe grain had to ripen as it stood in the sheaf after it had been cut. The sheaves were stood in stooks or kivers

(Cheshire word) for about three weeks, then carted and stacked. Our farm was short of shedding so Dad stacked both corn and hay out in the fields to speed up harvesting. This had a mixed success; grey squirrels in particular caused a lot of damage by eating into the thatch, which let in rain and did much damage.

The ground could be too wet to take the heavy steam engine and thrashing tackle to the stacks for most of the winter. A good frosty spell was needed to allow him to cross the fields to thrash his grain. On one of those occasions George Lea had been thrashing at our farm for most of the week, not finishing the last stack until late on Friday. With the ground frozen hard he had had no trouble moving from stack to stack and from field to field. He had a family commitment on the Saturday so he decided to leave his thrashing tackle where it stood until Monday. Unfortunately a thaw set in and by Monday the ground was so soft that his steam engine had sunk down to its axle. There was a winch on the engine but it was a long way from the nearest tree; it took him some hours to find enough chains to reach that tree and winch out the engine. It was the next day before he finally got all his tackle off the field.

A German pathfinder pilot got a bit confused one night and dropped his incendiary flares in a neat line down the middle of our farm. Harry was on Home Guard duty, so Eric went out with Dad to put them out. They were in no doubt that the flares were to pinpoint a bombing raid so when a German plane flew over they hid in the nearest ditch and when it had gone they ran out again. There were a few such panics

174

through the night but no more bombs were dropped. It was even more amazing that, considering the number of incendiary bombs dropped on the farm, no stacks were set alight. The flares were very hard to extinguish; when they had seemingly smothered them by digging soil onto them, they would burst into flames up to an hour later.

The bad experiences that Father had with his field stacks persuaded him to build a dutch barn. Of course there was quite a lot of red tape to go through, but finally permission was given and Dad built a five bay dutch barn. The open sides of a dutch barn meant that sheaves still had to be stacked with the same skill needed in building an ordinary stack outside, but there was no need either to build a steep roof or to thatch it. You just built up to the tin roof on top of the dutch barn, and if the rain came part way through the task, the roof protected the partly built stack.

Bombs did fall in the area but to my knowledge apart from the incendiaries, only one fell on our farm and that did not explode. When looking over stock one morning Harry found a hole where it appeared a bomb had landed, in the soft peaty soil on the big meadow. He reported it to Father, who reported it to the local police. They came to inspect the hole, agreed it was a bomb and reported it to the bomb disposal people. It was a mile walk from the farmyard to the bomb, so by the time all that had taken place it was late in the day by the time the bomb disposal experts got to the site. They inspected the hole and started to dig, but they

175

had only got about four foot down when it became too dark to carry on.

The next morning they returned to find their hole full of water, which made them pause for thought. Dad explained that that ground was full of water under the drains and that even if they dug a channel to either the nearby ditch or to an underground drain, below that level, without a pump, the hole would still fill with water. The army gave this more careful thought, pronounced that there was not a bomb there after all, filled their hole in and went away. Who can blame them, the Hall was the nearest building and that was more than a half mile away. Why bother splashing about in a remote field when there were so many other unexploded bombs to deal with in amongst homes and factories.

When Dad had moved to our farm he needed a loose box next to the stable, so that he could put a mare in when it started to foal. The Estate closed in a bay of the nearby cart house with the only material available in the war, which was rough but strong oak timber. No new windows could be had, and the only secondhand windows in stock at the estate yard were two lovely diamond pained multi-coloured stained glass ones. I never knew where they had originally been, but they looked very stylish over our loose box door. Later in the war a stray German bomber somewhat thoughtlessly, dropped a land mine on the next farm causing a lot of damage there. Although it was a mile from our farm, it blew out our two stained glass windows without doing any other damage to our buildings.

When an air raid was taking place we all went down to the cellar below the farm house. My parents had put some old beds in so we could sleep the night if need be. One of Father's uncles and two of his aunts had the same arrangement at their farm about two miles away. From the evidence, the experts said the bomb that killed them had hit the base of the house wall, right over the cellar. There was little found of either them or their possessions, nor was I left with all that much confidence in our cellar after that!

I will never forget one particular night that I spent down there. A couple of small bombs had exploded fairly close to the farm without doing any damage to our property, but they had rattled our nerves a bit. The rest of the family had got up to start the day and left me sleeping peacefully. I must have had a bad dream, I woke up in the pitch darkness convinced that they had all been killed. I will never forget the absolute terror that I felt; I was convinced that if I went up those stone steps I would find the house destroyed and my family all dead. I am told that I put my seven year old lungs to good effect.

Manchester was bombed just prior to Christmas with terrible devastation and loss of life. Some people headed out into the countryside, just anywhere to get away from the terror. One stranger came to our door on Christmas Eve, he had his two school age daughters in his small lorry with him. Of course Mum took them in and soon made up extra beds and some hot food. Then it got worse, because she collected up our four lots of Christmas presents and divided them into six — now that didn't seem too bad. Well, it didn't until she took my orange; I could not remember ever having had an orange before and was longing to taste one but Mum had only managed to buy two. I must have been a little horror because I am ashamed to admit that I kicked up quite a fuss, and in the end I got a clip behind the ear and was sent to bed. But I seem to remember having a super Christmas day with them and even being given a half of one orange.

Potatoes continued to dominate our farming life, not just in the summer months, because Dad stored them to supply his two or three regular customers through the whole year. I will come back to his growing and storing methods later in my story, when I was a little older so that I can describe the work involved. In those early years of the war it was all hand work, from carting the cow muck that grew them, to lifting and carting the crop. Father relied on Irish seasonal workers to do much of the hard graft, usually on some form of piecework scheme. This country has forgotten the debt we owe to Ireland; much of our increase in food production was both sown and harvested by those tough Irish lads. The seasonal workers came by boat to Liverpool and walked out from there to find work, often with no money to buy food or shelter. Many times one of them came into our farm looking for work after walking about forty miles from the boat without food.

Through those first few years at Toft, Dad had two regular Irishmen, both of whom left a lasting impression on me. The two of them lived in a shant in the back farm yard, where there was no running water, so a bucket of cold water was all they washed in. Many times in winter I saw them break the ice to wash in that bucket. There was a fireplace in the shant, but it wasn't worth lighting it to cook breakfast, so apart from a hot brew of tea from Mum, breakfast was cold. Those two tough old men, one aged sixty nine and the other seventy, could dig and bag four tons of potatoes in a day, just with forks and their hands. We were to have men getting potatoes with forks for another ten years or more, but I never saw any one beat that record.

In those days the local grocer called at the farm each Tuesday to take Mother's order and then delivered it on the Thursday, so it was no trouble for her to include an additional order for the two men. I carried it round to the shant one night to find one of them, Owdy O'Rourke, sitting by the fire. He had lost a leg below the knee whilst fighting for the British Army in India. After a day of hard graft on the farm his wooden leg must have chafed more than a little, so he had taken it off. It really was a wooden leg, just a round pole with a rubber cap on the bottom, and a leather cup on top. Two leather straps, nailed below the cup, looped round his leg to fasten above the knee.

When I put the groceries on the table, he hopped across the room to have a look in the box, just as light on his one foot as a five year old playing hopscotch. He loved to chat to me and whilst I stood by him a burning log rolled to the front of the fire, almost falling out. Owdy picked up his wooden leg and pushed the log

179

back on, then said with a chuckle, "I'll bet you can't do that, young John."

Whereas Owdy was a bit rough in his clothes, the other one of those two hardy old men, Martin McGuire, was always very clean and well dressed. As a young man he had worked both in England and America, but had returned to his homeland to choose a bride. He married on the understanding that they would make their home in this country; but alas it didn't work out. They set out to come to England but they only got to the station in Ireland. His young country-girl bride had never seen a train before and she refused to get on it. Martin worked out a compromise; he set up home on a small farm in Ireland, left his wife to run it, whilst he came over here to work.

His married life consisted of working for eleven months here, then returning home for one month each Christmas. I can't say if he ever spent more time than that at home when his children were young, and he managed to father six in his yearly visits. I do know that for most of the twenty years before working for Dad, he worked for Mr Whitter at Wheelock Hall on that basis. He retired from there intending to stay on his small farm from then on. Either the money was too tight or perhaps it was the shock of living with his wife for more than a month without a break. Whatever the reason, he came back here and took a job with Father. He had two married sons living and working over here, and in fact occasionally one or the other would stay with him on our farm.

Martin was with us about four years but Father would quote from his words of wisdom long after he had left. I honestly believe that Dad respected him more than any other person who had worked for him. Even I, as a young boy, remember him with the same respect. Not because he was full of fun, but he had a way of talking to me that always made what I had to say of importance. He always greeted me with a question like "Well, young John, how are you today?" More often it was, "What are you doing today, young John?" Even though he only had one hour in which to cook and eat his dinner, he would take time to listen to my answer and exchange more pleasantries.

Martin and Father would talk politics in some depth, and for many hours. On the serious side one of his topics was the Catholic Church in Ireland; he felt the church helped to keep his people poor. He illustrated it by the fact that when a farmer sold, say, a litter of pigs; the Priest was round the next day for a share of the proceeds. He felt the small Irish crofter was never left with enough money to improve his farm, and believed that the Church liked to keep them that way.

On the lighter side Martin loved to tell the story of when the land agent had called to see his old boss Mr Whitter. As it was just coming up to the mid-day meal time and as every tenant farmer liked to keep in with the agent, he was invited to stay. Martin was instructed to unharness the agent's pony from the trap, take it to the stable and feed it. That pony was used to being stall fed on dry hay and oats but Whitter's horses were at that time fed on freshly cut green grass. The pony

181

tucked in to this treat of fresh grass and ate more than was good for him; unfortunately not being used to it, it went through him like a dose of salts. After a long dinner the agent harnessed his pony and trotted smartly out of the yard. Before long the pony's tail came up and the green grass flowed out. It splashed on to the pony's legs, then on to its tail, which the pony did not like at all, so it started to flick its tail. By the time the smartly dressed agent had got back to his home, his tweed suit, polished brown shoes and the interior of the open front of the trap were all the same green colour.

CHAPTER
TEN

Odd Characters

1941 had seen a British success in the war, the desert campaign in Egypt led by General Wavell with some 70,000 men came up against the Italian's much larger army. As our troops swept forward the Italians surrendered in large numbers. I have not researched the figures involved but I seem to remember a staggering but vague one of hundreds of thousands of prisoners. Whatever the number, they caused a problem over here because we had to build many prisoner of war camps to hold them. It was decided that this vast army of men should be put to work. Without going in to the rules of what work a prisoner was allowed (or not allowed) to do, farming came out as the best option for them.

A large camp was built at Tarporly and from there Italian prisoners were carried out to the farms each day in enclosed lorries. Of course this was very time consuming and expensive so it was then decided to build a camp in Toft Park. The drive to the Hall passed through the main Park before crossing the stone bridge over the lake. The wire fence to enclose the prisoners was built on one side, the drive and the soldiers quarters on the other, leaving the drive over the bridge to the Hall still usable.

Father was asked to supply a horse and cart to work on the site each day. Harry took Jewel because she was the most patient of our horses when there was a lot of "standing around". Had Captain been used at the camp, he could be standing on three legs half asleep one minute, then if another cart rattled behind him, he could have been in the next parish a few minutes later. Prince needed to be working, he fretted when he had to stand for long periods waiting to be loaded or unloaded, and Harry found that there was a lot of that.

Harry described the workers building the camp as "the dregs of Liverpool". If he took his coat off and put it down it was stolen, if he tried to hurry any job on he was met with an uncooperative wall. On the farm Harry was used to working up to knocking off time, (with Dad he probably worked to five minutes after). On the camp they officially worked to 5 o'clock but were putting their tools away by 4 o'clock. Harry got caught out one afternoon with some bricks. Loaded onto his cart by one gang just before 4 o'clock, he was then stuck with them. Although it only took him five minutes to get them across the site to the builders, they were by then putting their tools away and refused to unload them. Harry was the most patient of people, but he had to threaten to tip the cart load of bricks into the partly built footing before they would agree to help.

Whilst Harry was working at the camp, my brother Arthur, although still at school, looked after and fed the other horses for him. Arthur always had a soft spot for

184

Prince and treated him to a few titbits extra. The result was that two weeks later when Harry wanted Prince to work, he had got so fat that he refused. Dad had had enough, his key man was away from the farm for days on end, so when Jack Cross moved in Dad sent him to the camp and kept Harry back to work at the farm. "Moved in" was the right description because Jack was one of those footloose men of past years who moved from farm to farm, living in the farm buildings whilst they earned enough for the next drinking session. I will come back to Jack Cross later in this chapter, but first I ought to explain more about his type, many of whom were part of the farming scene in those days.

The amount of handwork on farms, planting, weeding, hoeing and harvesting through the summer months, followed by hedge cutting and ditch cleaning in winter, provided casual work for the less fortunate. Each area had its own particular characters, men who could not hold down a full time job, perhaps because of infirmity or weakness. Often drink was at the bottom of their troubles; fortunately for them, many of those farm jobs could be done on piece work rates. If a man was paid a rate per score (twenty yards) to clean out a ditch, it didn't matter how slow he was. The fact that he had a hangover and didn't start until dinner time was of no concern to any one. The boss was usually happy to pay at stages as long the job got done eventually

Albert Howarth was another of those men. Drink had reduced his ability to work in more ways than one. The story was that he had been an educated smart young man and only started drinking after he had been

185

jilted. Three or four local farmers gave him a few light jobs from time to time, so he lived in the buildings belonging to whichever one might have some work.

In the depth of a bad winter before we moved to Toft, Albert had returned from the pub one night very drunk. Unfortunately he didn't quite make it right through the fodderbing doorway before collapsing into a drunken stupor, with his legs still outside. He was not found until after breakfast the next day, by when the severe frost had frozen his feet so solid that his boots had to be cut up to release them. I never knew just how much of each foot he had lost, but even when sober he could only totter along in a painfully unbalanced way.

Tramps were more common than today. Now the homeless are concentrated in small areas of the big cities. In my youth they were spread around the countryside, begging or doing odd jobs for a meal. There was seldom a week without at least one begging food or a night's rest in the buildings, two or three each week was the norm. My father may have been a hard man, but he never turned anyone away. At night he would always take their matches (so they couldn't burn the place down) and show them to the warmest spot. If they had not eaten, Mother would make up some food and send one of us kids out with it. Late in the evening it was often some "pobs", which was a bowl of broken bread filled with hot milk.

Sammy Tasker was one regular caller, but he was not really a tramp. His family were farmers and always kept him well-dressed and clean. He was in fact a good looking young man, until you looked into his eyes; they were chillingly vacant. It appeared that he would stay at home for some time and then just go on a walk about, calling at different farms on the way, sleeping over night wherever he had got to, and eating when someone took pity on him.

He was too simple to work (we didn't know what politically correct meant in those days) but he loved to plait horses' tails. He would just wander into the yard, walk across the cobbles to the stable and plait the tails of any horse in there — there was no asking if you wanted them plaited. Harry would sometimes go into the stable after a day's work in the fields, and find his resting horses neatly plaited, complete with ribbon. If there were no horse in the stable, Sammy would start on the cows; it was not uncommon to find five or six cows with a puzzled expression on their faces, each with the long hairs on the end of their tails neatly plaited, but because there was no ribbon in the shippens a bit of binder twine would make the bow on the bottom.

Mum would never allow me to wander around when Sammy was with us, but she never explained why. Even when she sent me out to take him a can of tea and a butty I was under strict orders to come straight back into the house. I can even remember her standing in the yard, waiting for my return. Perhaps those strange vacant eyes that fascinated me so much told Mum more than they told me.

When Sammy was around there was sometimes a colt left tied in the stable whilst the men were working

187

the other horses. Dad and Harry's method of breaking in colts was a fairly quiet slow process. Born in the spring, they would be ready to begin work in the late summer after their third birthday. Usually our colts had spent most of their lives, both summer and winter, in the big meadow. Well away from the farmyard, they were not touched or handled for months on end. Harry called them "raw colts", meaning green and untrained. He would bring them into the stable, tie them into a stall and stay with them until they accepted being fastened. As he fed and groomed his working horses he would talk to the colt, run his hands over its flank and slowly get it used to being handled.

When it was Blue's turn to be broken, she was not just a raw colt, she was also more nervous than most. Harry had to take great care when walking behind her, he never touched her from behind. In any event, he would never put his hand on to the rump of even a quiet colt; he would start at its neck, stroking and talking all the time, then slowly work along its flank. It could be days or even with the nervous type, a few weeks before he actually put his hand on one's rump.

After the "raw and nervous" Blue had only been in the stable a couple of days, Harry was more than a little surprised one afternoon to find her standing serene with a neatly plaited tail. Harry looked in the dark corners to see if there was a crumpled body, but in the end had to admit that Sammy with his simple mind had done what Harry, with years of experience would not have dared to do — stand just behind that colt and play about with her tail.

188

When Harry was happy that he could handle the colt, the first harness that he put on was a head collar with a special brass bit, which was used right through the breaking period. Brass was the most soft of metals and that training bit also had two toggles in the middle which encouraged the colt to play with them with her tongue. The colts constantly fiddling with those toggles kept the bit on the move in the mouth, which in turn toughened it to take the strong metal bit needed for later heavy work.

The next move was to just rest some harness on its back whilst talking to it. After a few days of that, he would harness the colt and leave it on whilst he fed and cleaned out the other horses, but he needed help to put the large neck collar on it. At that age those colts had reached their full height, but would need a year or two to fill out. If a colt of sixteen hands or more threw back its head, no one could reach up to put the heavy collar over it. Harry would get one of the other men to hold down on the bridle whilst he gently slid the collar over the massive head. It could only go over the head upside down and then be turned on the neck to rest properly on the colt's shoulders.

I was standing outside the stable door, watching Harry gently harnessing a young colt in its stall and I became fascinated with his skill. The stable was gloomy and in the stall it was too dark for me to see what he was doing. I kept moving a little closer to get a better view, and when Dad caught me I was right in the stable. I had been warned more than once not to go in and he was having a bad day. He just grabbed hold of my collar and dragged me out through the door and gave me an awful thrashing. No more explanations of how colts were prone to lash out, or the danger I put Harry in creeping round in the dark stable. He just raged as he slapped me hard across both ears and then on my bottom. It was cruel but I got the message that time.

The next stage in the colts' training was for Harry to lead it round the yards in full harness, then Dad led it whilst Harry drove it from behind with a pair of reins. They made the reins tickle and bump its legs, just as harness chains could when the colt would be pulling something. The colt jumped and shied in fear and surprise as the reins touched its flanks and legs and I got into trouble again for standing too close. Luckily Dad was busy hanging onto the dancing colt, so I got nothing more than a verbal.

Harry took that colt back to the stable for it to relax; it would then be brought out another day for the next stage. For that Dad had an old railway sleeper with a hook on one end; he explained to me how he and Harry would hitch the colt to it. At first they would lead it whilst it got used to the sleeper bumping along behind; when it settled to that they would then drive it with reins. From then on it was considered broken. Harry then worked it in the middle of a three horse team cultivating the autumn corn stubbles. When the corn had been cleared Dad always ploughed his stubbles with a light two furrowed plough designed to only plough about three inches deep. The idea was to encourage the weed seeds to germinate, then they could

190

be ploughed under with the winter ploughing. It was light and not exacting work, ideal for the colt to get the feel of hard work. The colt was only worked for half of each day at first, because it still needed more than a year to grow to full strength and gain the experience of a good working horse.

Every colt had a different time scale to each stage of breaking. The following year it was Bonny's turn and she was no trouble. I suspect that she had been a favourite from a foal and had been petted by every one. That could spoil some foals but Bonny loved it. I saw Harry putting her through some of the training stages with hardly a murmur. It is now over fifty years ago but Harry still remembers how easy she was to both train and work.

As waggoner Harry always checked on his horses before going to bed; many evenings he would spend a couple of hours in the stable just talking to or grooming them. Often he would then check round the cows for Dad, making sure they were comfortable and not short of food. One night he saw two cows looking hungry and went into the fodderbing with a pikel (pitch fork) to pitch some hay to them. In the dark shadows just as he was going to plunge his pikel into the loose hay, it moved, and out rolled a stuttering, spluttering skinny thin man.

It has taken me a long time to get back to Jack Cross, for it was he who rolled out of the hay. In the cold nights of winter he always slept curled in a ball and completely covered in loose hay. That episode was to be repeated many time through the following years. He

191

was part of my life for so long that now I have brought him into the story, I will not know where to break off. He would only be in his early thirties then, but like others the demon drink had destroyed his life and his physique until he looked an old man and was reduced to living in the fodderbing of any farm where there was some work. He became part of our lives, never reliable, he would only work for two or three days before the next drinking session. After each one he usually woke up in some other farm building, and he would then work there for a day or two before the same sequence took him further on, or back to us.

His brother then farmed their tenanted family farm near the Three Greyhounds in Allostock. As a young man Jack was the waggoner on Hulme Hall farm, Allostock, for many years. During that time, when out and about at dances or country shows he was always smartly dressed, with a gold watch chain across the front of his waistcoat. I never knew just what had happened; was it a girl? One rumour was that Jack had met his father when he was on his way to pay the half yearly rent. Between them they spent too much of it in the Three Greyhounds; Jack then took the rest on a long binge. I never believed it because I never knew Jack to do one dishonest act through all the years I was to know him.

Whatever the truth, Jack was reduced to the clothes he wore, which were one of each, union shirt, tweed jacket, trousers, overcoat and a pair of boots. No underclothes or socks, although I have seen him with stockings in winter. He was always clean and washed

192

his shirt regularly. His washday was the only time I ever heard Mum criticise him, because he always hung his shirt on her washing line for all to see. Mum kept her eye on the state of that shirt, when it got too holey she gave him one of Dad's. She had to get it just right though; if Mum gave him the replacement shirt before the other was really past wearing, Jack would keep the old one and sell the fresh one for a few drinks and then vanish for a few days.

His most treasured possession was an old bike. When he was sober he rode it, but when he had been drinking, he and the bike seemed to get equally drunk together. Usually we would see him coming down the footpath alongside the A50 just after afternoon closing time, Jack and the bike leaning against each other for mutual support. Jack's progress looked ungainly and uncoordinated but was highly practised, and his aim was to get to our farm for baggin time. When Mum saw him wobbling down the yard, she would smile, cut an extra butty and fill the tea can a bit fuller. Next morning Jack would be ready to work.

There was seldom a week without Jack staying with us some of the time; if there was no work on the farm he would always help each morning in winter to feed and bed down our cows and in return Mum always sent out a full cooked midday meal for him. When possible he liked to work on piecework rates and he would negotiate with Dad in his stuttering but articulate manner. I went with them to look at some rucks of muck that needed spreading. It had been hooked out of the horse cart with a long handled muck hook into piles

193

spaced at six paces apart. Dad had two sizes of rucks, one for a heavy dressing and a smaller for a light dressing on grassland. When we got to the field Dad was furious to see that the men had made those rucks too small and suggested that Jack should work for three half pence per ruck. Jack replied, "O-O-Owed on a-a minminute; if they'd b-b-bin too b-b-big you would'ner want to p-p-pay me any m-m-more, so I'll w-w-work for tuppence as u-u-usual!"

I went across the field with his baggin on the first day, and stopped to chat whilst he ate and drank. On the second day I did the same but noticed that Jack was stopping more often, just to stand fork in hand and look round. I told Dad when I got home, and he said, "That's a pity, I wanted him to finish that job before he went." Mum butted in "Well, there is nothing you can do about it, if he's started to look round he will be gone tonight"; and he was. He would come back two or three days, or maybe a week later; if the job wasn't finished, he would just carry on where he had left off. The muck had been spread so Dad paid Jack for what he had done without a cross word.

I was always surprised how tolerant Dad was with Old Jack; if anyone else let him down like that, Dad would order them off the farm and tell them not to come back. My parents always insisted that Jack was treated with tolerance and respect and in turn he had his own self respect. Through the summer months there was usually six to eight men working for Dad, occasionally some would tease Jack, and he did not like it one bit. I was with the men one day when Dad

194

caught two of them taking a rise out of Old Jack; they got the most vicious telling off, ending with "He's a better man than both of you will ever be". That couldn't have done much for their pride, but it illustrated just how much Dad thought of Old Jack.

For more than twenty years he was to spend each Christmas with us. No, I don't mean literally in the house. If he wasn't working for us beforehand, he would move into his favourite fodderbing one or two days before Christmas Day. Then on the day Dad would carve the meat onto Jack's plate first, Mum then piled it high with the other goodies and one of us would take it out to Jack. There was never any drink in our house, but that old soak chose to share his day with us regardless. Just one Christmas only did he fail to come and Mum worried and fretted for days, then he turned up without an explanation and stayed over the New Year.

Jack got me out of many scrapes, his kind guidance and wisdom saved me from Father's wrath a few times. The most memorable was after I had taken over the daily egg collection. I hated the job; free range hens were free range egg layers. Not only were there a lot of buildings and dutch barns, there were acres of nettles for them to lay in — well, it seemed like acres to me as I hunted for hens' nests in and around those three foot high nettlebeds. The egg numbers were falling, and Mum told me that I was missing some and I must try harder. I searched and searched, but if I found one new nest they deserted two others, even though I always left one egg to entice them back. Dad got to hear about the problem and made it clear that I had to collect more eggs or else!

I imagined those old hens deep in conversation round their nest one morning. First hen, "There was six eggs in that nest yesterday, now look there's only one." Second hen, "Perhaps it's rats." First hen, "No, it's that lad, I saw him creeping round after school last night." Third hen, "I hope he got his little legs nettled then." (I did too, many times.) Second hen, "We'll give him something to creep round after tonight, let's make a new nest." This they did, and where I couldn't find it. In the end I poured out my troubles to Jack. He just said, "W-W-We'll f-find um a-a-after b-b-breakfast S-S-Satdy m-m-morning."

After breakfast Jack was waiting for me, and away we went across the yard, as I thought to search the buildings and nettle beds. By then Dad still stacked most of his hay in the field where it grew, then had it baled with the big stationary baler that normally followed the thrasher. Those bales were eighty or ninety pounds each and Jack went straight to a pile of them in the dutch barn. I thought that he was going to look in the many gaps between them, but he just pulled one down, sat on one end and indicated for me to sit on the other and be quiet.

After about five minutes a hen started to cackle at the other end of the shed, Jack said, "There's one." We sat a little longer and another hen cackled behind the big dutch barn. I wanted to run round but Jack said "No." Soon another one said she had laid an egg, this time in a large nettle bed. There was over thirty eggs in that nest, twenty four in the first, but only five behind the dutch barn. I just had not thought that a hen cannot help but have a little chuckle each time it lays an egg. Old Jack had not only got me out of trouble, he taught me an important lesson in observation rather than dashing about.

Jack was the ideal man to work Jewel on the camp site, he didn't mind standing around, and as Harry said with wry humour, "he could put his jacket down without it being stolen." Jack supplemented Mum's big dinner with his own food at other meals. Before we got to know him, he had spent the summer months living under some large rhododendron bushes in the Moss Wood, where he learned to cook rabbit over an open stick fire. He only carried one snare; when I asked why, he replied, "t-then n-n-no one can say I'm p-p-poaching."

I loved to go with him to set that one snare. We took anything from a half hour to more than one hour. On the way he showed me the difference between a rabbit's slow feeding run and the faster travelling runs. Rabbits stick to their own runs and land in the same spot each time; that could be clearly seen by the depression in the grass. On the feeding runs they were nearly impossible to snare, because they were just hopping slowly in a more hunched position. Where they travelled fast to cross the field, the depressions were about two foot apart, and Jack would set his snare about four inches to one side of where the rabbit landed. He preferred a ditch-side run most of all. Again a rabbit lands and takes of from the same spot on each side of the ditch.

197

Jack set his snare just past where the rabbit's front feet touched down, its neck was then fully stretched forward and slipped into the noose. He also pointed out that a caught rabbit was more hidden from prying eyes down the side of a ditch.

With a few years difference between myself and my brothers, I had a lonely early life. We had no cousins near my age, and no neighbour's children to mix with; Dad would not allow other children onto the farm so I spent most of my time with the workmen. When Jack was in residence I was often with him, until the Italians came to work for us, then a new world opened up. At first they came each day just to pick potatoes, Mum would cook a massive dinner to feed our family of seven, plus two men living in, plus eight to ten Italians. The fact that the meat was often rabbit didn't stop them from enjoying a super helping, followed by apple pie or "beast custard" (made of cows' milk from the second milking after calving). When those were not available there was always the stand-by of stodgy rice pudding, but those men enjoyed that meal and were all kind and thoughtful to Mother and to me.

Mother's meals were always on time, so there was a good half hour to relax after dinner. I spent it with those chaps and one in particular asked me to help him learn English. He was a schoolteacher and said he may as well make use of the opportunity to learn our language. We used to sit in the garden, on the trunk of Dad's favourite Keswick apple tree. It had blown over, and had a prop put under which left the trunk flat enough to sit on, but it still grew lovely green eating apples.

Me teach him English! "Grief" — past tense, present tense, future. I did try, honestly, but he got me so confused that I still have not sorted out my has from an as. If any of you, when on holiday in Italy happened to meet a tall dignified schoolteacher, who speaks English with a broad Cheshire accent and seems a bit muddled on some of the simple parts of our language, you now know how it came about.

Dad and Mum were persuaded to have two Italian prisoners permanently on the farm. Of course it was necessary to be compatible if they were to share both our home and the work. The result was a series of trials, with different men staying a couple of weeks to see if they liked the job or Dad liked them. There was some funny events before it was over. One chap came to work in kid gloves and no way would he take them off. I never knew where he had manage to acquire such lovely gloves but it wasn't long before Dad told him where to take them to. Another, when helping with the milking, sat on his little three legged stool in the grouping behind the cow, milking away between its back legs. He found it hard to understand that although he may have milked his goats that way, our big cows were more likely to kick him through the back wall, or drown him from above!

Of course, all those instructions and conversation took place in very broken English. This was well illustrated to me the morning after Mickeal came to stay. He was a big, genial, always happy, Italian farmer whose broad smile was infectious. I trotted along on that first morning as Dad took him round the farmyard, stopping at different places to explain the work he would have to do. "Did you do this on your farm in Italy, Mickeal?" "No — Missus, she do this!" The reply was embellished with an elegant sweep of his arm. We went a little further to the next job and again Dad asked "Did you do this on your farm in Italy, Mickeal?" Again the same graceful sweep to emphasise that "Missus, she do!" This same charade was repeated a couple more times until Dad's patience snapped and he demanded. "What did you do on your farm in Italy?" "Ha, — me sit — veranda — rocking chair." All said with the most engaging grin that drew you to him like a magnet. After a few weeks Dad came to the conclusion that he must have been telling the truth, because he hadn't a clue about farming; his Missus must have been a very capable lady.

We finally settled down with two of the most delightful companions a war could throw up. A second Mickeal, (he taught us to pronounce it Mick-heal), was a medium built tough man in his thirties with the most fantastic tenor voice. He had the charm and charisma to go with it. Mum loved that man and fussed over him more than anyone. Where ever he was working his golden voice floated back across the fields; one elderly neighbour claimed to always spend her days in the garden if Mickeal was working near. She said that "there was nothing on the radio to equal him." When Mum wanted to know if he was coming home for tea, she would just stand out side and listen. Her eyes would light up when an operatic aria floated ever louder across the fields to her, as Mickeal's horse plodded its weary way home.

Mickeal was helping to fasten up some young cows. It was their first time in that shippen and they got a bit frisky. One ran backwards into Mickeal trapping him against the wall. He was in considerable pain from a couple of broken ribs, so Mum put him to bed and called in our Doctor. Whilst fussing over him in the most motherly way, she threatened my perplexed father as to what he would get if Mickeal had damaged his precious lungs. It was not just people; even the horses responded to him. Jewel would follow him round like a pet dog, nosing and touching him like a young lover out on a date.

I have heard people say that the Italians couldn't fight. I think they do that proud race an injustice. I was left with the strong impression that most of them disapproved strongly of both the war and the side that they were on, and had no intention of fighting us. One of those, a small Sicilian shepherd, Johnny, as everyone else called him, was no more than a boy of about twenty one when he was with us. He taught me to call him Jaykomo (with a soft J), Jaykomo Collottso. I never saw his name written down so my apologies to any Sicilian or Italian readers, but if any one knows a small crinkly-eyed quiet Sicilian shepherd with a name something like that, and who by now will be in his mid-seventies, I would love to hear from him

He had refused to fight, strongly believing that that war was wrong. Rather than join up he fled into the hills in Sicily. His family used to leave food out for him, but in the end they were forced to pass on the message that, if he did not enlist by a certain day, he would be "shot on sight". When he was telling me about that time and how he then enlisted, he added with both hands in the air and a broad grin on his face "funny thing, first time me see English, me get taken prisoner."

Our family at Finger Post lived, dined and played in the large kitchen. Mickeal and Jaykomo slept in the large bedroom up the back stairs and spent their evenings in the very large back kitchen. At one end of their kitchen was an open fire, blazing with logs through the winter months. A long wooden settee, two or three chairs, with a table for their meals, made up their furniture. When a group of them came for the day, there was enough space to put up a large trestle table that could seat twelve. The other end of the back kitchen had plate racks rising up from a wooden work bench to the ceiling, with dozens of large black pans on shelves underneath. A large stone sink with draining board stood between the outside door and the work bench. An electric cooker (after we had electricity) stood on the other side between the bench and the door into the kitchen. Electricity only came to our area when Toft camp was built, up to then we had used oil lamps or candles. If I remind you that there were also two large walk-through, stone shelved pantries, and that the main kitchen could also seat twelve around one large table, you get an idea just what a working farmhouse was like.

We children were normally only allowed one bath each week; on the other nights I washed in the stone sink. I have to admit some times I was just a bit economical with the water; Jaykomo would wag his finger, or in extreme times jump up and come to inspect behind my ears, muttering in Sicilian concern at my skimpy ablutions. I worshipped that delightful but untalkative companion. In winter he taught me to play draughts with the patience of a saint. If I made a wrong move, he just moved my piece back and tapped his forehead, which was his sign for me to think longer. Should I still make a rash move, he again returned my piece to its square and tapped again. I have to admit that sometimes that went on for a while, but slowly he taught me to think further and further ahead. It was to be many years before I realised just how well he had taught me. I played against a chap who claimed (Methodist ministers would tell the truth, wouldn't they?) to have played and beaten the champion of England. I was surprised that I managed to give him a good game and even cleaned up an odd time.

Recently I was fishing with my two brothers and got them talking about those times. I said that I could not understand why I had spent so much time with Jaykomo, where was Mickeal? They laughed and said I had been too young to understand; Mickeal had apparently spent his evenings out under the moonlight serenading Mum's daily help.

Some spring nights Jaykomo took me across the fields, not to walk far but to find a bank, where we could sit partially hidden behind a hedge or under a tree. "What are we looking for, Jaykomo?" He would just touch his lips with a sh—sh—, then touch his eye and give a sweeping point across the field. When a bird or a rabbit moved he just smiled and cautiously pointed. He never tried to explain or even discuss what we saw, but he taught me how to just sit and watch. On more recent holidays in Cyprus we motored into the hills. I sat with Celia under a Carab tree through the heat of the midday, and a small sun-wrinkled shepherd brought his flock to water. As the sheep and goats drank from the spring he sat relaxed, with far-seeing eyes gazing across the valley. He had the stillness of my old Sicilian friend. We had food and drink; eventually we left the shade of our tree to join him under his. We had no common language but shared our fruit with him. My thoughts went back to Jaykomo and the times he had just sat with that same stillness. Had he been sitting in the shade watching across his valley?

I came home from school one night to find him gone; no warning for him or me. I think they were moved up to the Orkneys, but it could have been the moon because I had no real name or address to write to. I was more heartbroken than I have ever been, before or since. I have recently visited the beautiful Italian Church on Orkney. The Italians were moved there to build the famous Churchill barriers across Scapa Flow. German U-Boats had slipped in to the deep water anchorage when our fleet was resting there, causing considerable damage and loss of life. The barriers blocked off several channels which made it easier to defend from a second attack. Whilst resting, those skilled and artistic men built a church. I stood in awe of the marvellous craftsmanship needed to convert two Nissen huts into a work of art. Again I felt close to that serene and delightful companion who I had the privilege to know for perhaps little more than twelve months — but twelve unforgettable months.

CHAPTER
ELEVEN

The Decoy

The plans to invade the Continent embroiled our little group of parishes in 1943, when General Patton set up headquarters at Toft and Over Peover. I am not sure if the Italian prisoners ever came to the Toft camp. If they did it was for only a few months before it was taken over by Patton to plan the invasion. Well, that was the story that was put out locally, and of course we were all very impressed that his two camps should be set up in our area, in fact just a half mile or so each side our farm.

The truth, as I understand it now, was completely different. Apparently General Patton had struck a soldier whom he had accused of cowardliness, and had been sent back from the front line in Africa in disgrace. But Hitler was still convinced that Patton was the top man; for him Eisenhower and Montgomery didn't really count. Hitler was so sure that the invasion would be led by Patton, that our leaders decided to build on his mistaken belief. The Allied forces decided to use General Patton as a decoy, to plan a mock invasion on the shortest route, an hour from Dover to Calais, whilst the real invasion was to be a six-hour journey going from Portsmouth, Southampton and the Isle of Wight, heading for Le Havre and Cherbourg.

Many Americans refuse to accept that the downfall of Patton ever took place; this is understandable because he played his decoy roll to perfection. He was given two or three hundred men who were housed at Toft Camp, whilst he and his senior staff stayed at Over Peover Hall. When he travelled from one camp to the other it was with, what we thought of at the time, overdone Yankie showmanship. Six or eight motorcycle outriders flanked his massive car, flags flew on top, traffic had to stop as he was driven with great pomp down the centre of the main road, past our farm, the one and a half miles between the two camps. It was ridiculous, but it was impressive, and it certainly could not but be noticed by any spying eyes; and of course that was the idea.

His men travelled around the North and East Midlands, even up as far as Yorkshire, sending impressive radio messages. Perhaps no more than two lorries, with just a few soldiers and plenty of radio equipment onboard, would pretend to be a convoy or even a regiment. I presume they sent messages like "One tank transporter has broken down; shall we stop the convoy or leave it and go on?" All those fake convoys eventually headed towards Essex, where large depots of equally fake plywood tanks and guns were gradually built up, carefully covered with sheets, as though they were the real thing being protected against the weather and spying eyes. They impressed the spy

207

planes and helped to convince Hitler that the invasion would go from Dover.

All those American troops created considerable movement along the A50; not just the Toft troops but other large convoys travelled past our farm. I discovered gum! I only had to sit on the hedge cop by the road when a convoy was on the move to collect a few packets. Mum got very upset; she said that I was begging; she wasn't going to have her son begging. I declared that I was just sitting watching the convoys go by (which sometimes could take upto an hour) and it wasn't my fault if some young American happened to throw me some gum.

Some of those young Americans were understandable homesick, and two or three soon discovered Mum's cooking. It was only a short walk across the park and a field to our home. Many if not most evenings we were joined by two or three of them. Their stay at Toft didn't last long, but friendships were formed that would last a life time. Mary has communicated with one of those Americans through the years, exchanging family news, photos of children, and more recently grandchildren, until his recent death.

Mother used to muse about the multi-national army she fed each day. Not only were there the Americans and our own staff, but two young German prisoners had replaced the Italians in our home. The older one Eric, was a dark-haired Hitler supporter. Although he was a willing worker he kept us at arm's length. Just once he got into a debate with Dad about Hitler. Father's debating skills were not too refined; he would listen to the other side, then say what he thought. If the other then restated the opposite view, he soon got mad. In broken English, Eric put his case, and of course Dad got mad! Fortunately Mum managed to separate them before they got to blows. As I remember it, Eric put forward a simple argument. "Before Hitler, in Germany, no work, no money. Hitler come, bring plenty work, plenty money." Dad must have found it hard to knock that simple fact down. The second prisoner, Stephen, was a tall, blond and blue-eyed, gentle carpenter, who soon replaced Jaykomo in my young life. He would never discuss politics or the war, but after we had both watched that heated debate I followed him out into the farmyard, where he turned to me and said, "Hitler no good!"

Again the two Germans spent their evenings in our back kitchen where Stephen brought a bit of German discipline to my evening ablutions. I not only had to wash behind my ears, I had to learn how to say it in German. My legs just above my knees and below my short trousers got very chapped in cold weather. Stephen was concerned because they were too sore for me to wash properly. He knocked on the kitchen door and asked Mum to come and look. Mum sent me off to the shippen where there was a big tin of Osmond's Udder Vac, a thick grease that was used for the same problem on cows' teats. It went on in a thick sticky paste, almost as bad as a fly paper. After putting it on, when I tried to turn over in bed I was stuck to the sheets; but it worked. On another occasion, when Stephen was supervising my evening wash, Eric spoke to him in German. I could only presume that Eric was telling him to mind his own business, whilst Stephen defended himself. It all got very heated, so I left them to it and fled upstairs to bed.

Stephen was a very accomplished wood carver. He searched around the big rhododendron bushes in the woods to find dead, dry seasoned branches for his carving. Just a length of branch held in one hand and a penknife in the other, he whittled away with amazing skill. He carved a Madonna for my sister Mary which she still treasures.

Then, again without warning to him or me, one breakfast time the guards came to collect him and Eric. Stephen left his breakfast unfinished on the table and went out to the old bakehouse workshop. Although Mum had tried hard to stop me from getting too attached to him, I had; so I trotted out to join him. He was whittling at a piece of wood and of course I started to snivel at losing yet another good friend. Stephen crouched before me, placed one hand on each of my shoulders to comfort me and I saw two big tears running down his cheeks; they did more for me than any words could. He then showed me his carving, it was a partially finished horse, and he was doing it for me! I rushed back into the house to tell them what was happening. The two guards kindly agreed to have a second cup of tea and a relaxed half-hour by the fire.

I have treasured that little carving all my life. It has lost both ears and part of one leg, but it still stands proudly on my mantelpiece. I always promised myself that some day I would carve a horse like it. It took me fifty years to get around to trying, but I did it. Alas mine, carved in horn, isn't Stephen's graceful thoroughbred, perhaps more like the half legged cart horse I described in earlier chapters, but I am thrilled with it and with the fact that he inspired me to start carving.

To help to further the mock invasion idea, General Eisenhower visited General Patton at his Over Peover HQ. They both took an evening out to travel down the cobbled stone lane and share a meal at the Bells of Peover Hotel (the hotel now attracts a few American tourists with that story). That is the kind of secret that soon spreads through a village, and the locals really did believe that they were to be part of history, and that the invasion and the end of the War was starting on our doorstep.

Although this is very much my version of those momentous events, I believe that Patton's decoy was so convincing that Hitler bought it, hook, line and sinker, to the extent that when the real invasion started Hitler was still convinced that it was the decoy, and kept his main army near Calais, waiting for the real invasion.

The story has an unusual twist, through Edgar Lea, the former miller at Lower Peover, who had taken a pub in Bangor before the War. He had volunteered for active service when the War started, but was turned down as too old. He had then been asked to take charge of an ordnance/munitions factory near there. He combined that job with running the pub. He was later put in charge of planning PLUTO (Pipe Line Under The Ocean), a bold plan to follow the invasion

211

across the sea with a pipeline to supply the petrol needed by the Allied forces as they advanced into France and Belgium. Many of his close relatives still don't know what he did through the War, believing that he just ran his pub in Wales. He had to pretend; it would have been ironic had he told any of his Lower Peover relatives his real role in the War. If when Patton and Eisenhower were having their carefully planned meal at the Bells, just one local smiled behind his pint and said "yes, but it's all a farce, our Edgar's planning the real invasion down at Poole in Dorset", all would have been lost and thousands or even hundreds of thousands of our troops would have died. Even the invasion itself may have failed.

Edgar only told his story after the War, and then only to his first cousin and close friend Wilfred Richardson who farmed at Lach Dennis. Wilfred caught polio and died in 1947 (at least eight members of our family have had polio), but his son Alan was there to hear the story from Edgar himself, and in turn to pass it on to me. Alan was a close friend of Edgar's son Roland. Roland joined Bomber Command and was lost over France.

If Edgar's story is correct (I have found no reason to doubt it), he played a major part in the invasion. Planning the fuel supply across to the Continent took a slice out of his life. In that time Kate his lovely wife, who before the War had turned the heads in Knutsford, turned a naval officer's head and ran off with him. Kate did return but I don't think they were ever really happy afterwards.

212

His son Roland, who at first was just reported lost, never returned. It was not until a few years after the War that his family found out what had happened to him. His plane had been shot down in rural France, the crew were all killed and Roland's body was buried by the partisans behind a hedge. When its position was re-discovered well after the War, it was dug up and reburied in Nantes cemetery. After the War, Edgar stayed in the south and worked for an oil company.

It seems strange looking back, that we were living in the North Midlands and yet preparations to invade the Continent were going on all around us. I could sit on a gate at the back of our stackyard and watch paratroops practising almost every afternoon when there was reasonable weather. The heavy, slow flying bomber planes took off from Ringway Airport (now Manchester International) and dropped the paratroops over Tatton Park close to Knutsford. As the crow flies, Tatton was no more than two miles from me, and although the dropping area in the park was hidden by distance and trees, I had a clear view of them as they practised speed disembarking. Dad leaned against the gate one afternoon as I sat watching plane load after plane load; from each circling plane parras were streaming out faster than I could count. Just as I was telling Dad that two had not opened properly, a third parachute failed to open at all. As the man plunged to the ground I turned to Dad in an excited schoolboy way, only to find him "as white as a sheet". He walked away disgusted with my boyish reactions at watching a man die.

213

Father had bought his first tractor, a standard Fordson. It had iron wheels with big spade lugs sticking out of the rear ones to gave it purchase on the soft soil. Eric Davies became the tractor driver and began then to take some of the skilled jobs away from his older brother, Harry. There were many jobs that could not be done with those first tractors. They had no hydraulic lift, so machinery could only be towed behind. Also the turning circle left a lot to be desired, which meant that the spring and summer work in amongst the growing root crops was still done with horses.

The heavy work such as ploughing and cultivating was slowly taken over by the tractor, as Dad gradually bought the different machines for each task. Perhaps the job that horses disliked more than any was pulling the heavy binder used to cut the corn. Not only was the machine heavy, but it was also wheel-driven; as the horse pulled it along a large iron wheel drove the complex mixture of sails, canvasses and binding equipment. If the dew was on the corn, the straw was sticky and it would cling and rap around the binder canvases, which meant that cutting could only take place through the heat of the day. It was a long continuous pull for the horses, with no natural break, just plodding round and round in the heat of the afternoon. The tractor could take that hard slog, without resting.

Three coal miners had persuaded Dad to let them come on the farm to shoot some of the rabbits living in the growing crops of corn. Each field of corn was cut from the outside, working round and round towards the middle, and rabbits often stayed in the uncut crop until little was left. Sport could be hectic when they broke, when thirty or forty rabbits could be shot in the last half hour of cutting. The coalminers got a bit carried away with the sport and more than once Eric had pellets pinging of his new tractor. Dad seemed to be putting up with the danger until they went too far. It happened at baggin time when one of the men called in the field with the food. As he was on his way to bring the dairy cows in for afternoon milking, the old collie dog was with him. Because of the danger from the binder, normally dogs were not allowed in the corn field at harvest time. The binder had stopped, the men were all gathering around the big can of tea and the food when the old dog went for a walk. He was just sniffing along the edge of the uncut wheat, when one of the miners saw the movement through the thin strip of wheat, and shot him. He lived for a few hours, even that would have been longer than the man who had shot him had Dad a gun in his hands just then.

The spade lug wheels prevented the tractor from going on the road so all road work was still left to Harry. Dad had bought a larger secondhand four-wheel lorry for this work. It was just over a ton in weight and could carry up to four tons of baled straw. Harry went to deliver a load to Tommy Ryley's farm at Mobberley with his usual team, which was Prince in the shafts and Jewel as chain horse. He had to go via the weighbridge at Knutsford station, which meant turning off the main road down Station Hill. The lorry and straw together made up a load of nearly five tons and as Harry led

Jewel into Station Hill, the weight was more than Prince could hold. There was a strong screw on the braking system, but the handle was halfway along the lorry, which meant the Harry had to run back to apply it. Whilst he was screwing the brake on Prince, desperately trying to keep his footing, slid into Jewel turning her sideways to the load. Harry rushed back to straighten her out, but the brake was not holding the lorry and old Prince was being pushed even faster. Had it been two young horses it would have been a disaster but Jewel responded and skipped back in front, letting Harry get back and give the brake another turn.

When Harry complained about the brakes, Dad would not accept that it was a problem and took the next load himself. Being aware of the problem he turned the brake on before the lorry went over the crown of the road, letting the horse pull it onto the hill. All went well until he got to Tommy Ryley's farm, where there was a steep bank up the drive and his faithful team just could not pull the load up. Dad walked up for help to Tommy's farm. Tommy's son Bert harnessed their horse and hooked it in front of Jewel, and the three horses managed to haul the straw up to the farm. Although Prince still looked well Dad began to realise that there was something wrong with him and got the vet out. When the vet had done a thorough examination, he shook his head sadly and Dad lost one of his treasured old team.

Delivering straw took Harry to some interesting places. One of his most memorable was only a half mile from the Finger Post. It was a small eight acre farm on which two elderly sisters kept five cows, a few hens and grew their own vegetables. There had been a brother, a tall man who walked with two sticks and always wore a bowler hat. He had never recovered from bad injuries received in the First World War and had died soon after we went to Toft. The Miss Baileys had Harry put his straw up into the hay loft above the cows. Those early bales were a struggle to get up through the small round pitch hole. The sisters helped as best they could, and when all the bales were in the loft they asked Harry would he like a drink. He wandered to the back door whilst the kettle was boiling and noticed the old cockerel standing on the kitchen table and taking sips out of a jug. Miss Bailey brushed it away with her hand and poured some milk into Harry's cup out off the same jug — Harry wandered around the farmyard mug in hand, waiting for the chance to tip it away when they were not looking.

One of the sisters used to "tent" (abbreviation of tend) the cows along the Seven Sisters Lane each Summer day. On our walk to Sunday School we would stop and talk to her as the cows munched among the wild flowers on the road side. When a car came, which wasn't very often, she would guide the cows out of the way, stroking them gently, and they would respond by licking her hand. Their living must have been frugal; poverty showed in their clothes. Harry said their stockings had "so many holes they looked like wire netting."

Their mode of talk was from the turn of the century, very feminine, fluttery, even girlish and shy. I was with

Dad one day when one of them came across the field. She was trying to get him away from me in her fluttery way. I was curious and stayed near but Dad eventually got the message and sent me away. It concerned one of their cows; having become so close to them, the cows saw the Miss Baileys has one of them. When cows come on heat they respond to nature by riding each other, (today's farmers watch for this to know when to AI them). One of Miss Bailey's found it quite normal to try to ride Miss Bailey. I have often wondered how she managed to find the genteel words to explain the problem to Father, but a visit from our bull soon put the matter right.

With a new tractor on the farm, Father's horse power had changed and, from being short of horses in the early years, Dad had now got a surplus. The Blue colt and Bonny were working well, and there was a younger colt coming on, so Dad decided to sell one or two horses. Mr Alan Smith came all the way from Rochdale to look at Blue, watched Harry ploughing with her (in a team of three) but rejected her on the grounds that he wanted her for town work and she was not yet five years old. Maybe he detected that nervous streak and made her age an excuse to say no! Dick Willett bought Judy back again, obviously he was not worried about her tendency to jib occasionally after a few days rest.

Captain attracted the interest of a farmer whose farm lay just by the runway at Ringway. I think Dad was happy to see him go; not only could he take flight on the odd occasion, he could still lash out if someone touched his rump unexpectedly. On one occasion

Captain had kicked the curry comb out of Harry's hand; but those were the type of quirks that many horses had — they were all declared to the buyer. Dad was more than a little surprised to have the buyer complain, over a month after he had bought him, that Captain wouldn't work. Dad and Harry went to see Captain and his new owner on their farm by the runway at Ringway Airport. They were surprised to find the farm under armed guard; armed soldiers asked their business, some were even sitting in the hay loft covering them with rifles. In the end they were allowed into the farm, where they found Captain standing in the stable. The farmer was not at home so they asked his workman if there was any work for Captain to do.

"Yes, there was hay needing turning." Harry soon had Captain harnessed and out in the field. Those old hay turners rattled and clanged but Captain was on his best behaviour, working steadily for about two hours, until at last the workman came and took over from Harry. All that time Dad had wandered around the farmyard or walked back and to the field, waiting for Captain's owner to return. When he did finally come home, he soon agreed that the horse was a good worker (he had been trying to bluff Dad into giving some money back) — end of story. Well, no, it wasn't, because those troops guarding the airport and the paratroops practising for D-Day had become very suspicious of Dad. They held him and Harry at gunpoint and would not let them leave. I think Harry enjoyed seeing his boss at the end of a gun barrel, trying to talk his way out of a tough situation. In the

219

end they managed to convince the guards of their innocence and were released.

It was not the only time that Harry found himself at the wrong end of a gun barrel. In between Home Guard duties and overtime on the farm, he attended Knutsford Young Farmers Club. They arranged a mixture of educational and entertaining evenings. The club was invited by Lord Egerton's farm bailiff to visit the Home Farm at Tatton. The farm's arable land was around three sides of the large park — the same park that was the dropping zone for parachute training. The Young Farmers had been given clear instructions as to which part of the park was out of bounds because of the paras, but knowing young farmers of today, I have no doubt that they were just the same then. Rather than listening to instructions, most of them would be busy flirting or perhaps planning where they could escape to. Whatever the reason, the two car loads of young farmers wandered into the wrong area and were suddenly surrounded by armed soldiers. There was no politeness; guns were pointed at them in no uncertain way and they were marched away and locked up. It was after midnight before they managed to convince the paratroops that their visit to the training area was completely innocent.

In those later years of the War, the country was drained of raw materials; everything that could have been used for the war effort had been. Timber was in short supply, and Jim Gough was under constant pressure to fell trees in the most inaccessible places. He looks back with pride to the ash trees he felled for the doors and bomb hatches on the Lancaster bombers that dropped the bouncing bombs, now made famous by the "Dam Busters" film. Ash was the best wood to stand the force caused when each heavy bomb was released. The bomb's weight caused a whiplash effect that could break more ridged timber, but ash is flexible and springy and withstood the shock.

Jim was asked to fell a stand of timber in a very steep ravine at Ruabon near to Corwen in North Wales. The terrain was so steep that two other timber men had refused to take on the job. Jim set about those tall trees with a gang of seven, two Welshmen and five Italian prisoners. The tree trunks were 120 ft long when fallen, and they had to cut them into two 60ft lengths to haul them away. By then he was equipped with an Austin pole waggon — after horses and steam engines it seemed like the very latest in technology to him.

It took several months to clear that one stand of timber, and during that time Jim and his team lived with various local families. One farmer in particular, whose land they had to cross with their heavy tackle, had put up with considerable inconvenience and damage from them, so it came of no surprise when Jim was asked to help kill the farm pig. Jim had plenty of experience back in his school days behind Mrs Cragg's little shop, so he thought it was the least he could do in return for the problems he had caused the farmer.

During the food rationing each farm was allowed to kill two pigs each year, strictly on a licence, for their own use only. Farmers soon realised that a pig was a pig regardless of size, so they grew them on and on

221

until they were as large as the proverbial donkey. When Jim got to that isolated old, stone-built farmhouse, he was not surprised to find a massive pig standing quietly in the yard. What did surprise him was that they planned to slaughter it in the farm kitchen. With the heavy table pushed to one side and the Welsh dresser standing on the other, there was a good space in the middle of the Welsh slate floor. Jim pointed out the size of the pig compared to the large step, going up through a fairly narrow doorway in to the kitchen. To which the old farmer laughed and said "we ain't carrying it in." The farmer's daughter had fed it from a weanling and had made a pet of the pig, so she just talked it in to the kitchen. There was no humane killer so it was still a throat-slitting job; it took four strong men to wrestle it down and hold it still so that it couldn't damage the furniture with its dying kicks. The daughter calmly swilled the blood out through the door, perhaps a little sad, but stalwartly accepting the loss of her pet.

Pigs were not skinned, the bristly hair was softened by lying the pig in a massive shallow tub of near boiling water, then scraped off with an implement that was almost like a short handled hoe. It took three or four hours of hard work to kill, scald, scrape the hair off and then clean out a large pig. When they had finished the daughter gave the floor a last swill out, the men washed their hands, and Mum pushed the big table back into the middle of the kitchen and served up a hearty farm tea on the very spot where the pig had a little earlier kicked its last. That was the sort of comradeship that was part of everyday life throughout the War.

222

Suddenly it was all change around our farm; not only did the two German prisoners Eric and Stephen leave, but the Americans left at the same time. The camp was now used for what it had been originally built for, a prisoner of war camp. The Allied Forces were at last on their way across the Channel on June 6th 1944. Edgar Lea's part in the planning worked; PLUTO was a success, and the pipeline was floated out on large wooden reels. They were unrolled like large floating cotton bobbins, with the oil pipe dropping onto the sea floor. Reaching from Southampton to Cherbourg it was in use within days, supplying the fuel to keep our forces going until later when they could freely open up the port of Antwerp.

When the Allied forces landed and started to fight their way inland, the German generals asked for reinforcements; but Hitler said "No!" General Patton's decoy had worked. Hitler was still so convinced that the action was just a feint that he held back his main armoured force for what he thought would be the real battle against Patton. History shows just how valuable those first ten or twelve days were. By the time Hitler realised his mistake the Allies had landed nearly two million troops, had a secure base in France and were on their way towards Belgium.

Geoff Gough, now a corporal, had finished his training to take his place in the invasion and went over in the second week, landing just west of Cherbourg, almost behind Caen. He was with the 61st Medium Denbighshire Yeomanry Regiment, Royal Artillery, and in fact was to stay with them until the regiment broke up in March 1946. Having lost their guns at Dunkirk the regiment was now fully equipped with new 5.5inch medium guns pulled by AEC Matadore Tractors, each the size of a bus. There were 16 guns to the regiment, 8 to a battery, 4 guns to a troop and 2 to a section, and the regiment could be broken down to fire in any of those divisions. Mostly they fought as two batteries; the 243 was the Colwyn Bay Battery, and the 244 was the Wrexham. Throughout the campaign, Geoff's battery was to fire 42,000 rounds and the other 40,000, each of those shells weighing 80 lbs.

They were core troops and were sent wherever their big guns were needed. Geoff was soon promoted to sergeant and has kept a meticulous record of the campaign. His Colonel had all the regiment's records but unfortunately when he died, his widow must have been fed up with the sight of them and burnt them all. Geoff's records remain and will some day go into the regiment's history — my very short mention of his war does not do either him or his regiment justice.

Geoff recalls how the German army collapsed in France. In the Falaise area they were almost encircled. Our forces pounded them from three sides causing chaos and destruction on a vast scale. Our men were surprised to find that the progressive German Army was dependent on the heavy horse. Many of its heavy guns were pulled with horses and its supply columns were based on horse transport. Many of those heavy horses were caught in the fighting. The carnage was so great after the battle, there was so many dead horses and troops that Geoff found he could not always tell men from horses. Bulldozers had to be used to collect and bury them together in the quarries at Saint Contest — the white stone from whose quarries.many of our cathedrals are built.

Our troops moved fast from Normandy, because the German army did not stand and fight until they reached the Dutch border. The PLUTO pipeline followed them, now underground as far as Lisieux from where it supplied the fuel for the Allied troops until Antwerp was in operation in October 1944.

One incident that I picked out from his records took place near the German border. Our troops had been instructed to get to the Baltic Sea before the Russians, to stop them getting round it and into Denmark. As they rushed forward they were held up by what turned out to be a detachment of German Youth. Geoff and his guns were ordered in to break the impasse, but it was not without a fight and during the battle Geoff was under machine gun fire from the youths. They were finally captured with help from the infantry and Geoff's battery were horrified to find that they had been fighting boys only twelve to fourteen years old. Many of Geoff's soldiers had children older than them back at home. But a bullet fired by a young boy still travels at the same speed!

The German officer leading those boys had a camera with him; Geoff took charge of it and took several pictures from the front line to add colour to his carefully kept journal. Geoff received a citation for

225

bravery, but in his modest way he joked, "You could either have that or two hundred cigarettes and when it got to my turn all the cigs had gone."

CHAPTER
TWELVE

The War Comes to An End

Eric Davies had left our farm. He enjoyed his tractor driving but on the farm there were many other jobs which kept him away from the tractor seat. His new job was with his two step-brothers, working one of their sets of thrashing tackle. He enjoyed being responsible for the maintenance of the thrashing machinery, and meeting people as he drove from farm to farm. But the thrasher created a lot of dust and dirt, and many of his generation have been left with the chest problems caused by the corn dust around the thrasher.

George, my oldest brother, left school and took over some of the tractor driving work, but Dad shared it around. Arthur though still at school seemed to spend a lot of time on the tractor. Dad replaced his first Fordson with a new one, which had a set of rubber tyres as well as the spade lug iron ones. The lack of versatility in those early tractors meant that the horse was still the means of power for all the skilled work around the many acres of root crops.

My book seems to full of stories of horse problems; either running away or lashing out at someone. In the working life of a waggoner those events were few and far between, and there were days and weeks of quiet, enjoyable work. Harry loved the work that took him in to the fields day after day, especially when Jewel was with him. They had become so used to each other through the years together that he could work her without reins. He could tell her to work either on top of the drill, when half splitting to bury muck or cover newly planted seed, or in the bottom when working in the growing crops.

Jewel placed her feet so neatly down each drill, not damaging the young potato plants as she walked back and to, through the long day. Her colt Blue inherited that same neat foot work but whereas Jewel worked untroubled without reins right up to the main road, George, who usually worked Blue, found that she was always nervous near traffic. Occasionally a heavy lorry would make an extra bump or rattle and Blue would whip round in panic. She never actually ran away from him, but a few times she ended up next to George, facing backwards down the next drill. George would have to swing her back round to the front or unhitch her to get both the horse, the chains and the swindle tree back in line with the scarifier, all of which, in the process, broke off a few young potato plants.

Potatoes demanded a lot of attention if they were to be kept relatively weed free. In wet summers the soil could be too wet to work for long spells without compacting it, then weeds were almost impossible to

228

keep down. Nowadays weed-suppressing chemicals are a boon to the arable farmer. There were drill harrows to knock the weeds off the top of the drills before the potato plants were up; then a scarifier to cultivate in between each drill, and the job was finished by drawing up the drill again with a drill plough, hopefully smothering most of the weeds. All those jobs were still done by horses; the harrows could do two drills at once but the others were a drill at a time, each needing a single horse and of course a man to walk behind guiding the scarifier or drill plough between the growing crop.

Two men (at times three) with their horses worked whenever the ground was dry enough for cultivation. It was a never-ending battle to keep the weeds down. Other than Sunday, everyday right through from mid-March into June they followed their horse up and down each drill. When wet weather stopped those jobs for a spell, perhaps letting the potatoes grow too big to harrow the top of the drill off without damaging them, then the rest of the farm staff would have to do the same job with hoes or forks. The men had to hand-hoe in both the turnip and mangel crops anyway. Weeding and thinning the young plants, leaving one plant every 10 inches, was a time consuming task each May, followed by a second or even third weeding in June.

Father grew most of his potatoes for particular customers. Mrs Copestick with her chip shops in the Potteries demanded different varieties to Mr Hutson who had two or three greengrocer shops in Altrincham and Sale. The list of varieties in his record book for

1941 read like this: May Queen, 1 acre; Ninety Fold, 5 acres; Arran Pilot, 1 acre; Scotch Guard, 1 acre; Arran Banner, 1 acre; Doon Star, 2 acres; Majestic, 2 acres; Red Skin, 2 acres; Gladstone, 4 acres. What lovely old names — with a catchy tune one could make them into a song. Later in the War he increased the acres but dropped one or two varieties. The different varieties were grown so that he could both sell some straight off the field for immediate use in the summer months, and store the rest to keep his regular customers supplied all the year round. The surplus was taken to Knutsford station and put on a train for Manchester Market, where an agent sold them and would pay Dad the market price less his commission. After we lost Prince, Harry made the journey to Knutsford station four days a week in the potato harvesting period with Jewel in the shafts and Blue as chain horse. He walked with Blue on the way in, but on the return journey he tied her behind the empty lorry, and sat on the front whilst Jewel plodded her weary way home. At first Blue didn't like the traffic and started to push with her chest against the back of the lorry; on one occasion she pushed the lorry and Jewel all the way home, arriving there covered in lather from fear and effort.

The labour needed to grow that many potatoes was considerable, not just weeding and harvesting, but in preparation and planting. It was basically "organic" production but after the ground had been worked, fertilizer was broadcast before it was drawn up into drills. Cow muck was then spread along the bottom of each drill by hand. After Dad had a tractor the muck

230

was no longer tipped into rucks to be spread later with a fork, but was carted out by tractor trailer. The driver and two men loaded each load with forks, then in the field the tractor was driven slowly down the drills whilst the other two men threw the muck into three drills on each side of the trailer. The muck did not land evenly enough for Father, so other men then knocked it along to make a level continuous line along the bottom of each drill. Harry or another skilled waggoner would then "half split" each drill with horse and drill plough, covering the muck with just an inch or two of soil. The potatoes were then planted on that soil just above the rich farmyard manure, and finally they were covered with horse and drill plough, leaving a lovely smooth pointed drill.

As you can imagine, it took almost an army to do all that hand work, and Father had an army. Toft Camp was by then the only international camp in the country, housing POWs from the countries that Germany had over-run, men who had been forced into German uniform. Just as the Roman army two thousand years ago had been a multi-national force drawn from the many countries within the Roman Empire — of course always led by true Romans — so the German army built up a similar force. Reluctant conscripts from occupied countries were mixed in with the Fatherland troops, led by ruthless German officers. Czechoslovakia, Hungary, Yugoslavia, Bulgaria, Austria and Romania were the main sources and in turn they made up the bulk of the POWs at Toft. There were many other nationalities. Whatever their circumstances or reasons, if the War had overrun them, they were gathered up and mercilessly used.

In case you think that they could or should have refused to wear uniform, let me tell you about just three or four of them. Although many of their names have been forgotten through the years, their experiences have stayed imprinted on my mind. Others stayed after the War, found work, married and became part of our community. Each had a story of brutal horror, fear and suffering to tell. One Romanian, whose name now escapes me, told how he and his sister lived on a small farm with two aunts and his uncle. When they were both in their late teens the German army came with two covered lorries. His sister was told to get into one lorry and he into the other. The girls were being collected to "entertain" the occupying troops. The old folks began to object and argue with the soldiers. The boy was forced to climb into the other lorry, and as it drove out of the little farmyard, he saw his uncle and two aunts lined up against the stable wall, there was a burst of gunfire and they all three slumped on to the cobbled yard. That was his lasting memory of his family.

Two Hungarian boys who worked for Dad were taken from the same village school when one was only twelve and the other fourteen. How could they say "No" when told to wear German uniform? It was the end of the War before either of them had any news from home, then the oldest one received his first letter from home telling him that his mother and one sister were still alive. He came to work that morning with the letter in his hand, and went straight to the farmhouse to tell my parents. The emotion was just too much for him. I watched as Mother cradled him in her arms, rocking him gently whilst he sobbed and sobbed. The news that he still had some family left alive was too much to contain, it completely overwhelmed him.

Wenzel Spatschek was only twelve when Germany overran Czechoslovakia. A large force stopped at his little village of Lytany, near to Pilzen (where the beer comes from). Many villagers were forced out of their homes and the village to make way for German families, but Wenzel's parents were allowed to stay. The fact that he had a Czech father and a German mother saved them and because of it he was presumed good material for the future German empire. Wenzel went to a German school — it was still in the same building but from then on he was a German schoolboy.

Wenzel's call up was more conventional. He stayed at school until he was fourteen and then was allowed to do a three-year blacksmith apprenticeship before being called up at seventeen. Before going into the army he had three fascinating years working with the village blacksmith doing all sorts of metal work, but mostly shoeing. The small farmers from Wenzel's youth often relied on a bullock or even their old milk cow to do their farmwork. The cow would be milked in the early morning, then harnessed up to work in the field or pull a small cart through the day. I asked Wenzel if they weren't a bit slow for work. He replied. "So what, I grew up in an age when time wasn't so important; what was not done one day, could be done the next" — said

233

with a lovely European gesture of splayed hands. When walking, cattle have a habit of throwing their front feet out and slightly sideways as they touch the ground; that meant that the outside claw of a working cow would wear from constant walking. To prevent this the blacksmith made a small D-shaped shoe for each outside claw on the front feet. Care had to be taken when nailing the shoe on, and very fine nails used as a cow's foot has not got the large horny area that a horse's has.

Wenzel described how it took two men to train a bullock or cow to work in harness, very much in the way that Harry and Dad broke in our colts, but the two men would have a rope from either side of the cow to stop the sudden head-down runaway charge that cattle can make. The big difference was that the small farms had so little space around them that the training was done through the village streets for all to watch. The village had the trunk of a small tree to hitch the cow or bullock to, then with the two handlers to hold and guide it, the log was dragged back and to through the village. This was repeated for several days, until the cow or bullock became trustworthy in harness.

In 1943 at the age of seventeen, Wenzel was sent by train into Germany for training. The army did not make use of his blacksmith's training but put him to work with horses. After four weeks he was sent to the French coast as part of the German defence force. Stationed just outside Cherbourg he was part of the force that met our invasion. Geoff Gough described the carnage of the German army — well, Wenzel was amongst that carnage, in charge of six horses pulling a heavy gun. In the action he was ordered to move his gun forward. He rode on the front left horse, guiding the others with his right hand. A British plane dropped a bomb so close that it lifted the horses off the ground. When a second bomb dropped nearly as close, he lost all control of them, as they bucked and leaped in a frenzy of fear. Thrown to the ground Wenzel landed on his feet and he kept on running; he was soon joined by two other horsemen who had done the same. When they got back to their HQ an officer asked about their guns. They told him, "they have been captured".

The German army were already surrounded so it wasn't long before Wenzel got the chance to slip away. He just walked down a narrow country lane and surrendered to the Canadian force. Transferred to the British Force he was stripped of all his clothes (which were burnt), then deloused in a room filled with gas and given a new uniform with a half moon crescent on the back. Fred spent many months helping to clean up behind our lines, mostly collecting and burying the dead. Eventually interrogations established that he was not a volunteer and as he was not a German national he was sent to Toft. The Toft POWs were expected to work, and most of them wanted to. Fred volunteered to do farmwork and was sent to Tom Bell at Ullard Hall Farm, behind the camp. We British not only fail to learn other languages but we can't even pronounce a hint of a foreign name; the Bell family soon called Wenzel a more simple "Fred", and that name has stuck with him throughout his life.

The road journey from the camp to the farm was about two miles; the walk through the fields was only a half mile, so Fred asked if he could walk. He and the Bell family became good friends. Although the POWs were not allowed any British money, just camp coupons, Tom Bell gave Fred a little, to treat both himself and a few friends each weekend. The most hated British guard was nicknamed Sergeant Kramer. Responsible for preventing the POWs from bringing in anything from outside, he did his job diligently. Fred usually arrived back from his work completely on his own, but each time he had to report to the guard house. Kramer had become suspicious that he might be carrying money so he was made to strip. Fred had slipped his money into his socks, so he stripped down to them, standing naked before the Sergeant. Kramer said "I will have the socks as well." Fred carefully slipped each sock off in turn, managing to leave the money on the floor under both feet without it being noticed!

On our farm we had the same group of four or five young men through a few years. Mostly Hungarians, they had each been through Hell and back and were glad that it was over. They would walk to our farm each morning, arriving ready and willing to work. Many of them were country boys, and some had not worn boots until they went into the army; so as soon as they got into the field their shoes and socks came off, and I was fascinated by how broad their feet were. Not having worn boots to restrict their growth, their feet had spread until it must have been hard to find boots to fit them. They could chase rabbits over the sharp spiky cut stubble at harvest time, or back over thistles in the potato drills without a thought of pain.

Whenever I was at home in the daytime I would try to be with them, fascinated by everything about them. Some were only in their late teens, but mostly in their twenties, they were full of fun and good humour. To our own farm staff, most jobs were repetitive hard graft, but those energetic and fit companions turned each task into a competition. Who could pick the most potatoes, pitch sheaves of corn the faster, mow quickest with a scythe; whatever they had to do was done with that spirit of fun. Baggin time was a chance to challenge each other at weight-lifting or to wrestle together; bare backs would rub against the rough ground with disdain. Luis was one of my favourites, he was nearly as broad across his shoulders as he was high. He changed our rope swing under a dutch barn for a trapeze made from the chains and bar of a chain-horse harness. The old style dutch barn was built on brick pillars and the trapeze was fastened to a wooden beam in the roof. Each lunch hour tested that old barn to its limit, it creaked and groaned whilst the trapeze swung up to near horizontal. Sometimes taking no notice of the jagged machinery parked underneath they would challenge each other to feats of daring.

On the first warm day of spring, Luis took his shirt off and only heavy rain or numbing cold could make him put it on again. He didn't bother to get acclimatized to the sun or use any sort of sun cream; the result, some really large blisters more than an inch across. Mum provided some sort of healing ointment which Luis had me rub on his broad muscular back each day, but he still stripped to the waist. The following spring he did just the same again.

At busy times in the year, extra numbers would come to help with the corn harvest or potato picking. Then, as with the Italians, one would willingly help Mum with the vegetables. They all treated each meal as a special occasion, sometimes carrying the trestle table outside to enjoy the fickle British summer. Those men had been carefully selected because of their suffering at the hands of the Germans. It was no surprise then, for all their good humour, that when one of them noticed a Nazi SS tattoo on one man's arm when he was in the shower at the camp, he was killed on the spot. It happened during a school holiday and I was told not to ask them any questions about the incident.

When I was about ten my parents moved me to the Egerton School in Knutsford. My brothers were teasing me through the summer holidays about how I would have to fight each member of the dreaded Moor Gang. Knutsford is built on an incline and the Moor Gang came from the bottom side of the town. Being the youngest of the family I had never really learned to fight — how can you fight someone five years older. Not having played with other children, I had gone to infant school ill prepared to defend myself and I must admit that I was bullied. I had no intention of ever being bullied again, so I got a bit worried. The POWs heard this teasing and asked me to explain. When I did they went into a little conference and appointed a trainer for me, a tough, craggy-faced, reserved man of about five foot nine or ten, and a little older than the rest of them. If this were a novel I would invent a tough sounding name and give him a colourful past, but it is real life and I just cannot remember anything about him, not even his nationality. He was only with us for about two or three weeks. I had already noticed that the others treated him with respect and deference, whilst he treated their youthful antics with an indulgent smile.

His English was very bad; he was only able to speak a few broken words as he took me into the workshop after lunch. It was only very basic stuff: lead with my left, tuck my right elbow in, keep my right fist up, but it made me feel a big man. Mum became suspicious as to what we were doing and came in to see. He said, pointing at me, "he teach . . . me . . . English."

The next day he took me out of sight behind the workshop. He started that next lesson by saying "fight . . . in . . . here," tapping his forehead, "go . . . in . . . hard." Then after struggling to find the right words he illustrated what he was trying to say with expressive continental gestures; he managed to convey that if I frightened the other fellow at the start, I could have the fight already won. Holding his hands up for me to hit he dodged about pretending to fight. When I led with my left, he said "no poke . . . punch" — this enforced with a hard punch with his left fist into his right palm, all the time encouraging me to hit his hands, then with mock pain saying "you . . . got . . . good punch." Although it was only three or four fifteen-minute sessions, it did an immense amount for my confidence, and it illustrates the bond that we all had with those young men who shared our lives for that brief period.

I had been at my new school for over a week before I met the so-called Moor Gang. Playing with a group of other boys by the wall at the back of the school playground, suddenly they were all gone. I looked about in puzzlement and realised that closing in on me was a group of about eight boys who formed a half circle around me, with the wall at my back. Warrell, the leader, had been sent down from the class above and was about two years older than me. Although he was no taller, he had broad muscular shoulders that made quite a dent in my new-found confidence. He calmly said, "We've come to see who you can fight . . ."

They seemed to be arranged in order of merit, Warrell in the centre, his lieutenant next, then decreasing in size towards each end of the half circle. I was too scared to take in or remember the exact words, but he indicated that I was to start at the smallest and fight each one in turn. I must have showed my reluctance to that idea; well, the smallest looked a tough little beggar and might have given me a whipping. Warrell then said "well, you can't fight me!" When his lieutenant repeated the same words I thought "why not?" He was nearer my age and build, so with "you . . . got . . . good punch" to boost my confidence, I did what the man said and went straight for him.

I suppose that I learned one of the important lessons in life that lunch hour. No matter how afraid I was underneath, if I could hide it, I could bluff it out. I seem to remember landing one punch, the rest of the time I was flailing fresh air. Warrell caught us up about halfway across the playground. He said, "well, you can fight him — but you can't fight me." I managed to stand my ground and look him in the eye but I must admit that I was too frightened to speak; I just waited for him to hit me. He really was an amazing boy, there was no shouting or fist waving, he just stood calmly in front of me. Thankfully he must have taken my petrified silence as some sort of manly agreement and suddenly turned and walked away. Throughout my year at that school I never once saw him do a mean act; if any of his gang got into a fight, he would see that it was fair, no boots or ganging up on anyone. As for me, I never had a wrong word with any of them, so fortunately I never really found out if my tough boxing tutor had taught me anything.

Our forces were closing in on Hitler, bomb raids were almost a thing of the past. Then in those dying months of the War we had our most frightening experience. It happened when Dad was up and going to bring the dairy herd in for milking at about six in the morning. He had walked across the stack yard to open the field gate when a flying bomb came low and straight towards the house. Its speed was not fast (in terms of today's rocket speeds) so Dad ran back towards his home. He realised that it would beat him and stopped by his new dutch barn horrified as the "doogle bug" headed for the house.

The noise was as frightening as the sight. Dad, convinced that it would hit and wipe out his whole family, leaned against the corner upright girder of the

241

dutch barn for support. Even it shook with the vibration. He swore that it passed between the tall chimney pots, missing the roof by no more than a foot or two. I was fast asleep in bed and was woken by that terrifying noise — I thought that a tractor was on the roof. Every slate rattled and shook with the vibration, but it was gone in a moment and I can remember laying there completely bewildered. The ground slopes away from Toft towards the Peover Eye and the River Dane, and allowed it to fly on for a few more miles before crashing and exploding between Middlewich and Northwich. A second one dropped less than a mile short of our farm in a field in Ollerton. People came from miles away just to look at the crater left by the explosion.

The War was over at last, but other than the relief, particularly that no more lives would be lost, changes came slowly. The POWs were still prisoners under guard at the camp but they could each try to get more news from home. Fred was thrilled to hear that his parents were still alive and living in the same village. He applied to the authorities in Czechoslovakia for permission to return home but it was to be many months before he heard. By that time Tom and Edith Bell had offered him a home and full time job on their farm. He took it and has the proud achievement off being the first prisoner to leave the camp.

His new job was not without incident though; within a few days of starting he had to clean out the shippen. Each farm had a muck midden in the yard which could gradually build up to become quite high. Planks of wood, each about a foot wide were placed end to end, so that the men could push their wheel-barrow full of muck right up on to the top. The planks were always greasy and Fred was trying to show his new boss how fast he could work. He can still laugh about going head first into the proverbial.

Tom Bell's bull was not to be trusted. Because of his nasty nature he was tied with two neck chains. Even so he managed to break both and escaped. The bull got through the wood on to our big meadow, chased by Tom and his staff each armed with a pikel. Fred was young and fit so he managed to get ahead of the others and when the bull crashed through the fence back into the wood Fred was just behind him. By that time the bull was getting a bit fed up with being chased and spun round to have ago. Fred dropped the pikel and leapt up the nearest tree, only avoiding the bull's horns by inches. The bull put his head to the small tree trunk and shook it, but Fred held on grimly. In the end Tom Bell decided to try a different method and turned ten cows out to join the bull, and by the next day he had settled down and they were able to take him in with the cows without endangering anyone's life.

When Fred started that job he had no idea just how long it would last. At first as a single youth he lived in with the family, but later when he married a farmer's daughter, part of the large farmhouse was converted into a flat for them. After some years they managed to build a bungalow on his wife's home farm, but Fred worked on for the Bell family for forty five years. It was many years before Fred was able to return to the little village of Lytany, and it was heartbreaking to see it. German families had settled there during the War, in the Czechoslovakian homes and small farms vacated by the persecuted Czechs. After the War they in turn were driven out of the village. Fred was dismayed to find large parts of his village derelict. Where once families had lived and children had played, the houses were empty, decaying shells. The small farms that were the heart of their thriving community had been amalgamated into one large soulless collective farm. Fred did go back once again to a village reunion. People returned from all over Europe, some sporting Swiss Alpine hats, others in Bavarian shorts, most revealing in their clothes something of their new identity and country. The one thing in common was their sadness at the sight of their village and childhood homes. Very few allowed nostalgia to overcome good sense in returning home to live under Communist rule!

The War was over for Geoff Gough, having crossed the Rhine and got well into Germany by the time Montgomery received the German surrender at Luneberg Heath in May 1945. He wasn't allowed to come home; there was a lot of clearing up to do in Germany. Later, when his regiment was broken up in 1946, Geoff was the longest serving non-commissioned officer.

The War was over for my family on the farm, but again life went on the same. Food rationing, not just for humans, but also for our livestock still controlled our business life. But peace was wonderful. No more awful news stories, no more reports of the loss of friends or relatives and no more bombs in the night.

We worshipped at Ollerton Chapel, just a mile from our farm, where we children went to morning and afternoon Sunday School, then often back at 6.30 to evening service. I presume that my parents wanted to share that thanksgiving with friends from their past. Whatever the reason, we went to a thanksgiving service in Bradshaw Brook Chapel. The chapel was full, the hymns were sung with fervour and the door had to be left open to let in some fresh air. Dad's old friend John Clarkson sat in his usual place near the front and as usual when the door was left open, his old collie dog wandered in and lay moaning with boredom in the isle by his pew. Although I was too young then to understand faith, that little country chapel was to play an important part in my life. As I got a little older I used to cycle there to join in with the other young people, playing table tennis, cricket, football; perhaps even girls drew me there. When at the age of twenty I lay completely paralysed, I found that along the way I had developed a faith upon which I could rely; no one can ask for more.

Also available in the
ISIS Large Print Reminiscence Series:

Thistle Soup

Peter Kerr

"A brimming and lively broth of rural characters, drunken ghosts, bullocks in bedrooms and country superstitions." **From the bestselling author of Snowball Oranges**

East Lothian is "The Garden of Scotland" and the setting of this delightfully idiosyncratic story of country life. Often hilarious, always heartfelt and at times sad, here unfold the ups and downs of four generations of one farming family in this amazing landscape.

Young Peter Kerr, the peedie boy who sets his heart on filling his somewhat eccentric grandfather's straw-lined wellies, grows up to run the family farm which puts his ability to see the funny side of things to good use, as adversities crop up with an intriguing regularity.

ISBN 0-7531-7145-7 (hb)
ISBN 0-7531-7146-5 (pb)

By Hook and By Crook

Fred Archer

". . . a valuable and fascinating account of life as truly lived in a village under Bredon Hill." **Sunday Times**

In William Archer's day, corn was reaped in August by hook and by crook — just one stage in the unending cycle of tying and stooking, gleaning and stone-clearing, harrowing and replanting. But there was time enough for William to become shin-kicking champion at the Bredon Games, and for a travelling Russian and his dancing bear to give some pig thieves a fright in the night.

Fred Archer remembers all these tales from his grandfather, farming during the long reign of Queen Victoria. He remembers his Uncle Jim, the old Ashton Squires, the hunting parson, and villagers like Jim Dance, the Squire's groom, with his ready remedies for the fluke and the husk in sheep and cattle.

With the warmth and humour for which he is highly regarded, Fred Archer brings us the true voice from the livelier English peasantry in the Vale of Evesham.

ISBN 0-7531-9962-9 (hb)
ISBN 0-7531-9963-7 (pb)